FOUNDATION BUSINESS MATHEMATICS

Series Editor
Brian Coyle

i

PASSWORD FOUNDATION BUSINESS MATHEMATICS

First edition January 1990

ISBN 1 871824 05 2

Published by
BPP Publishing Ltd
BPP House, Aldine Place,
142/144 Uxbridge Road, London W12 8AA

Printed by Dotesios Printers Ltd, Trowbridge

A CIP Catalogue reference for this book
is available from the British Library

CONTENTS

PREFACE

Password is a series of multiple choice question books on business and accountancy topics. If you are studying for an examination, or would just like to test your knowledge on one of these topics, Password books have two special features which are designed to help you.

1 They contain about 300 multiple choice questions, with answers provided later in the book. You can get an objective idea of your strengths and weaknesses, and whether your standard is as high as you would like it to be.

2 We explain most solutions in some detail, to show why one answer is correct and the others are wrong. Our comments should help you to learn from any mistakes you have made, and to improve your understanding of the subject.

Objective testing is an increasingly popular method of examination. An answer is right or wrong, and there are no 'grey areas' or 'in-between answers' that are half-right or arguably correct. Multiple choice questions (MCQs) are the form of objective testing that is now most widely used. Professional bodies that have adopted MCQs for some examination papers include the Institute of Chartered Accountants in England and Wales, the Institute of Chartered Accountants of Scotland and the Chartered Institute of Management Accountants. The Chartered Association of Certified Accountants has recently taken a first step in the same direction.

MCQs offer much more than exam practice, though. They test your knowledge and understanding. And they help with learning.

- The brevity of the questions, and having to select a correct answer from four choices (A, B, C or D), makes them convenient to use. You can do some on your journey to or from work or college on the train or the bus.

- We know from experience that many people like MCQs, find them fun and enjoy the opportunity to mark their own answers exactly.

- Being short, MCQs are able collectively to cover every aspect of a topic area. They make you realise what you know and what you don't.

If you're looking for the fun and challenge of self-testing, or preparing for an examination - not just a multiple choice exam - Password is designed to help you. You can check your own standard, monitor your progress, spot your own weaknesses, and learn things that you hadn't picked up from your text-book or study manual. Most important, Password books allow you to find out for yourself how good you are at a topic, and how much better you want to be.

Good luck!

Brian Coyle
January 1990

PASSWORD. MULTIPLE CHOICE

HOW TO USE THIS BOOK

Aims of the book

This book is designed:

- to familiarise you with a type of question that you are increasingly likely to face if you are studying for examinations.

- to develop your knowledge of Business Mathematics through repeated practice on questions covering all areas of the subject. There are about 300 questions in this book.

The multiple choice approach

A multiple choice question is in two parts.

- The *stem* sets out the problem or task to be solved. It may be in the form of a question, or it may be an unfinished statement which has to be completed.

- The *options* are the possible responses from which you must choose the one you believe to be correct. There is only one correct option (called the *key*); the other, incorrect, options are called *distractors*.

There are various ways in which you may be asked to indicate your chosen response. If you meet with MCQs in an examination, you should obviously read the instructions carefully. In this book, you will find that the options are identified by the letters A, B, C, D. To indicate your choice, draw a circle round the letter you have chosen.

The notes

In Section 1 of this book each chapter begins with brief notes which are designed to refresh your memory of the subject area and get you thinking along the right lines before you begin to tackle the questions.

The notes are *not* a substitute for a textbook: Password assumes that you are already broadly familiar with the topics covered in the chapter. Nor do they give you answers to all the questions.

- The notes are a *reminder* of the key points in each topic area. If your studies have left you feeling that you can't see the wood for the trees, the notes may help to bring the important issues into focus.

- They provide brief *guidance* on particularly knotty points or areas which often cause problems for students.

The questions

The questions are arranged roughly in the order of the key areas highlighted by the notes. But it is difficult, and undesirable, to keep topics completely separate: there's a great deal of overlapping.

The general principle has been for questions *on each topic* to get progressively harder. The result of this is that within a single chapter the level of difficulty will rise, and then fall back to begin rising again. So if you have trouble with two or three questions, don't assume that you have to give up on the whole chapter: there may be easier questions ahead!

If you can, try to work through a whole chapter before turning to the solutions. If you refer to the marking schedule after each question you will find it almost impossible to avoid seeing the answer to the next question, and the value of the book will be lessened.

However, chapters vary in length. Some are quite short, but others are very long. We have taken the view that there is no point in dividing up longer chapters into two just for the sake of making chapters shorter, and so some chapters contain over 50 questions. In these cases you might decide to tackle the questions in a chapter in several different sessions, over a period of time, and check your answers at the end of each session.

Finally, don't rush your answers. Distractors are exactly what their name suggests: they are meant to look plausible and distract you from the correct option. Unless you are absolutely certain you know the answer, look carefully at each option in turn before making your choice. You will need a calculator and a pen, and paper for rough workings would be helpful, although you could use the blank space on each page for any rough workings that you need to do.

The marking schedules

The marking schedules indicate the correct answer to each question and the number of marks available. You should add up the marks on all the questions you got right and compare your total with the maximum marks available.

At the foot of each marking schedule there is a rating, which is intended to be helpful in indicating the amount of work you still need to do on each topic. You'll need to use your discretion in interpreting your rating, though. The book may be used by a very wide range of readers, from college students and students of professional, business and accountancy courses, to qualified managers with years of practical experience. A mark of 10 out of 35 might be worryingly low for an experienced person, while representing a very creditable achievement for someone at an earlier stage of his studies.

The comments

The answers to purely factual questions generally need no explanation, but for most questions there is a commentary or a numerical solution, usually set out in some detail.

These comments will usually describe why a particular option is correct and (more commonly) set out the calculations leading to the correct answer. Distractors are usually chosen to illustrate common misconceptions, or plausible, but incorrect, lines of calculation. The comments will often highlight what is wrong about particular distractors and this should help in clarifying your ideas about topics that you may have misunderstood.

Conclusion

Password Foundation Business Mathematics is designed as an aid both to learning and to revision. It is not primarily aimed at those who are already expert in the subject. So don't expect to score 100%. And don't despair if your marks seem relatively low. Choosing the wrong answer to a question is not a failure, if by studying the solution and comments you learn something you did not know before. This is particularly relevant if you are using the book at an early stage in your studies, rather than in the final stages of revision.

And if you *do* score 100%? There are 14 other Password titles to get through...

SECTION 1
NOTES AND QUESTIONS

CHAPTER 1

BASIC MATHEMATICS

This chapter covers the following topics:

- Arithmetic
- Roots and indices
- Factorials
- Arithmetic progressions
- Geometric progressions
- Simultaneous equations
- Quadratic equations
- Matrices
- Linear programming

1.   Arithmetic

1.1   While this book covers a wide range of topics, we will start with a revision of the basics. It is worthwhile making sure that you are completely happy with basic mathematics, as it is a skill that will pay off time and again throughout this book.

1.2   We start with the key rules for the basic operations of addition, subtraction, multiplication and division.

1.3   We have rules to tell us which order to work things out in.

> (a)   Do things in brackets before doing things outside them:
> $(7 + 4) \times 5 = 11 \times 5 = 55$.
>
> (b)   Subject to rule (a), do multiplications and divisions before additions and subtractions:
> $3 + 2 \times 8 = 3 + 16 = 19$

Example:
$$
\begin{aligned}
&(3 + 8) \times 4 \;-(6 + 2 \times 5)\; -7 \times 2 \;-1\\
=\;&\quad 11 \times 4 \;-(6 + 10)\quad -14 \quad -1\\
=\;&\quad\quad 44 \;-16 \quad\quad\quad -14 \quad -1\\
=\;&\quad\quad 13
\end{aligned}
$$

1.4 If you multiply or divide a pair of numbers, and they are both positive or both negative, the answer is positive. If one is positive and the other is negative, the answer is negative.

$$-3 \times -2 = 6 \qquad\qquad -4 \div -2 = 2$$
$$-3 \times 2 = -6 \qquad\qquad -4 \div 2 = -2$$

2. Roots and indices

2.1 The square root of a number is the value which, when multiplied by itself, equals the original number:

$$\sqrt{16} = 4, \text{ since } 4 \times 4 = 16$$

2.2 Similarly, the cube root of a number is the value which, when multiplied by itself twice, equals the original number:

$$\sqrt[3]{27} = 3, \text{ since } 3 \times 3 \times 3 = 27$$

2.3 The nth root of a number is the value which, when multiplied by itself (n - 1) times, equals the original number:

$$\sqrt[8]{256} = 2, \text{ since } 2 \times 2 \times 2 \times 2 \times 2 \times 2 \times 2 \times 2 = 256.$$

2.4 'Powers' work the other way round. The little number is called an index (plural indices).

Thus $2^8 = 256$
and $3^3 = 27$
and $4^2 = 16$

2.5 When a number with an index is multiplied by the *same* number with the same or a different index, the answer (the product) is found by adding together the indices.

(a) $y^2 \times y^4 = y^{(2+4)} = y^6$

(b) $3^5 \times 3^3 = 3^{(5+3)} = 3^8 = 6,561$

2.6 When a number with an index is divided by the *same* number with the same or a different index, the second index is subtracted from the first index:

(a) $p^7 \div p^3 = p^{(7-3)} = p^4$

(b) $7^6 \div 7^3 = 7^{(6-3)} = 7^3 = 343$

2.7 An index can be a fraction, eg $16^{\frac{1}{2}}$. This means the square root of 16.

Similarly, $125^{\frac{1}{3}}$ $=$ $\sqrt[3]{125}$ $= 5$

and $81^{\frac{1}{4}}$ $=$ $\sqrt[4]{81}$ $= 3$

2.8 An index can be a negative value. The negative sign represents a 'reciprocal' or 'one over':

(a) 2^{-2} $=$ $\frac{1}{2^2}$ $=$ $\frac{1}{4}$

(b) 6^{-3} $=$ $\frac{1}{6^3}$ $=$ $\frac{1}{216}$

(c) y^{-7} $=$ $\frac{1}{y^7}$

2.9 You can get an index of zero:

12^0 $= 1$

$(-57)^0$ $= 1$

x^0 $= 1$

Any number to the power 0 equals 1.

3. Factorials

3.1 The factorial of a number is that number, multiplied by each number lower than it down to 1. It is denoted with an exclamation mark. For instance

$$5! = 5 \times 4 \times 3 \times 2 \times 1 = 120$$

3.2 Some time can be saved when dividing factorials. Consider the following example:

$$\frac{16!}{12!} = \frac{16 \times 15 \times 14 \times 13 \times 12 \dots\dots\dots \times 1}{12 \times 11 \times 10 \times 9 \times 8 \times\dots\dots\dots\times 1}$$

This could be simplified to $\dfrac{16 \times 15 \times 14 \times 13 \times 12!}{12!}$

Cancel the 12! $= 16 \times 15 \times 14 \times 13$
                   $= 43,680$

3.3 0! is defined to equal 1.

4. Arithmetic progressions (series)

4.1 An arithmetic progression is a series in which there is a constant, or common difference between successive terms. For example:

   (a)   in the arithmetic progression   3, 10, 17, 24, 31, the common difference is 7
   (b)   in the arithmetic progression   45, 39, 33, 27, 21, the common difference is -6

4.2 | The nth term in an arithmetic progression is given by $(a + (n - 1)d)$
     |
     | where   a is the first term in the progression
     | d is the common difference

4.3 | The sum of the first n terms in an arithmetic progression (S_n)
     |
     | is given by $S_n = \frac{n}{2}(a + z)$
     |
     | where z, the nth term, $= (a + (n - 1)d)$

5. Geometric progressions (series)

5.1 A geometric progression is a series in which there is a common or constant ratio between successive terms. For example:

   (a)   in the geometric progression   2, 10, 50, 250, the common ratio is 5
   (b)   in the geometric progression   200, 100, 50, 25, the common ratio is 0.5

5.2 | The nth term in a geometric progression is given by
     |
     | $ar^{(n - 1)}$
     |
     | where   a is the first term in the progression
     | r is the common ratio

5.3 | The sum of the first n terms in a geometric progression (S_n) is given by
     |
     | $S_n = \frac{a(1 - r^n)}{(1 - r)}$

5.4 When there is an infinite geometric progression, and r is less than 1, the sum of the terms will have a finite value.

> The sum of the infinite geometric progression, where r is less than 1 $= \dfrac{a}{1-r}$

6. Simultaneous equations

6.1 Simultaneous equations are two or more equations which involve several unknown variables which we have to find values for. For simultaneous equations to be solved, there must be as many equations as there are unknown variables. For example, to find the values of three variables, x, y and z, we need three different simultaneous equations containing x, y and z.

6.2 We solve them by multiplying equations by constants, until we get one term (for example, 3x) in two equations. Subtracting one equation from the other then gets rid of that term, and we eventually get an equation in one unknown, which we can solve.

7. Quadratic equations

7.1 Quadratic equations can be expressed in the form $ax^2 + bx + c = 0$. We are given values for a, b and c, and x is the unknown variable. Nearly every quadratic equation has two values of x, called roots of the equation, which satisfy the equation. That is, if we put either root back into $ax^2 + bx + c$, and work it out, we get 0.

7.2 Quadratic equations can be solved by two methods:

- by factorising the equation
- by using a formula.

7.3 Factorising is breaking down into two terms which, when multiplied together, yield the original equation. For instance

if $x^2 - 7x + 12 = 0$

this equation can be factorised as

$(x - 4)(x - 3) = 0$

(Check for yourself that, if you multiply out the brackets, you arrive back at the original equation.)

Since $(x - 4)(x - 3) = 0$,
either $\quad x - 4 = 0 \quad \therefore x = 4$
or $\quad x - 3 = 0 \quad \therefore x = 3$

7.4 Alternatively, the two values of x can be found using the following formula, which you should learn:

$$\text{If} \quad ax^2 + bx + c = 0$$

$$x = \frac{-b \pm \sqrt{b^2 - 4ac}}{2a}$$

In the example in paragraph 7.3, using the formula:

$$x = \frac{-(-7) \pm \sqrt{(-7)^2 - (4)(1)(12)}}{2(1)}$$

$$= \frac{7 \pm \sqrt{49 - 48}}{2} = \frac{7 + 1}{2} \text{ or } \frac{7 - 1}{2} = 4 \text{ or } 3$$

8. Matrices

8.1 A matrix (plural: matrices) is simply a set of numbers arranged in a table such as

$$\begin{pmatrix} 1 & 4 & 7 \\ 2 & 6 & -8 \end{pmatrix}$$

This is a matrix with 2 rows and 3 columns, and so is a 2 x 3 matrix.

8.2 We can multiply two matrices so long as the first matrix has as many columns as the second has rows. Take each row of the first matrix, turn it through $90°$ clockwise so it becomes a column, and imagine it put next to each column of the second matrix in turn. The numbers side by side, one in the column derived from a row of the first matrix and one in the column of the second matrix, are then multiplied. The results of these multiplications are then added to give a figure in the product. Check carefully that you can follow the workings in the example below w, where a (2 x 2) matrix is multiplied by another (2 x 2) matrix.

$$\begin{pmatrix} 3 & 4 \\ -1 & -6 \end{pmatrix} \begin{pmatrix} 2 & 6 \\ 1 & 2 \end{pmatrix} = \begin{pmatrix} 3 \times 2 + 4 \times 1 & 3 \times 6 + 4 \times 2 \\ -1 \times 2 - 6 \times 1 & -1 \times 6 - 6 \times 2 \end{pmatrix} = \begin{pmatrix} 10 & 26 \\ -8 & -18 \end{pmatrix}$$

8.3 A matrix with ones in every place on the diagonal from top left to bottom right (the main diagonal) and zeros everywhere else is an *identity matrix*. If you multiply it by any other matrix, the result is the same as that other matrix.

8.4 The *inverse of a matrix* (let's call it matrix A) is the matrix which, when multiplied by that first matrix A, gives the identity matrix. The inverse of a matrix A is denoted A^{-1}

$$\text{If } A = \begin{pmatrix} a & b \\ c & d \end{pmatrix}, \quad A^{-1} = \frac{1}{ad - bc} \begin{pmatrix} d & -b \\ -c & a \end{pmatrix}$$

Example: if $A = \begin{pmatrix} 8 & 3 \\ 2 & 1 \end{pmatrix}$,

$$A^{-1} = \frac{1}{8 \times 1 - 2 \times 3} \begin{pmatrix} 1 & -3 \\ -2 & 8 \end{pmatrix} = \frac{1}{2} \begin{pmatrix} 1 & -3 \\ -2 & 8 \end{pmatrix} = \begin{pmatrix} 0.5 & -1.5 \\ -1 & 4 \end{pmatrix}$$

8.5 Simultaneous equations can be expressed with matrices:

$$3x + 2y = 11$$
$$7x + 4y = 23$$

can be expressed as

$$\begin{pmatrix} 3 & 2 \\ 7 & 4 \end{pmatrix} \begin{pmatrix} x \\ y \end{pmatrix} = \begin{pmatrix} 11 \\ 23 \end{pmatrix}$$

9. Linear programming

9.1 Linear programming may be in the syllabus you are studying for. If it is, you should learn it from your study text. These brief notes are intended as memory-joggers, to bring the key points to mind.

9.2 Linear programming is a technique to allocate scarce resources, usually so as to maximise profit or minimise costs.

9.3 The essential elements in a linear programming problem are:

- A definition of variables, such as x = number of red pens made and y = number of black pens made

- An objective, such as to maximise contribution to profits, where contribution = $3x + 2y$

- The constraints, such as
$$3x + 2y \leqslant 10{,}000$$
$$x + y \leqslant 7{,}000$$
$$x \geqslant 500$$

- A graph, showing each of the constraints as a straight line and a feasible region (the possible values of x and y)

- Identification of the best point(s) in the feasible region (always a corner, or two corners plus the edge joining them), ie the point(s) where our objective (maximum contribution, for example) is achieved.

9.4 You will find examples of this method in the questions.

QUESTIONS

1 2 + 7 x 5 - (-3 + 1) equals

A 35
B 39
C 47
D 72

Circle your answer

A   B   C   D

2 -3 x 4 + (-2 x -1) -7 x (-2) + 3 x 8 equals

A 10
B 14
C 24
D 28

Circle your answer

A   B   C   D

3 3^3 x 2^3 + 5^2 x 5^2 + 385^0 equals

A 751
B 842
C 1,135
D 1,226

Circle your answer

A   B   C   D

4 The fraction $\dfrac{x^8}{x^4}$ equals

A 2
B 4
C x^2
D x^4

Circle your answer

A   B   C   D

5 If $y^{\frac{1}{3}} = x^3 - 3x^2 + 22x - 156.5$, what is the value of y when x = 5?

A 12.25
B 20.25
C 42.875
D 91.125

Circle your answer

A   B   C   D

6 If x = -3 and y = 2, which of the following inequalities is correct?

A $-y^2 > 2xy > x^3$

B $2xy < -y^2 < x^3$

C $2xy > x^3 > -y^2$

D $x^3 < -y^2 < 2xy$

Circle your answer

A   B   C   D

7 x^{-3} equals

A $\sqrt[3]{x}$

B $\dfrac{1}{x^3}$

C $\dfrac{1}{\sqrt[3]{x}}$

D $-x^3$

Circle your answer

A   B   C   D

8 $3^{-6} \div 3^{-2}$ equals

A $\dfrac{1}{6,561}$

B $\dfrac{1}{81}$

C $\dfrac{1}{27}$

D 9

Circle your answer

A   B   C   D

9 $\dfrac{27!}{24!3!}$ equals

A 0.375
B 1.000
C 2,925
D 17,550

Circle your answer

| A | B | C | D |

10 $\dfrac{30!\ 3!}{0!\ 27!}$ equals

A 5,220
B 73,080
C 146,160
D 3,946,320

Circle your answer

| A | B | C | D |

Data for questions 11 and 12

Reade Limited have just commenced production of a new product. The number of units produced during the first week was 600. The managers expect weekly production will increase by 20 units each week for the next 15 weeks.

11 How many units will be produced in the fifteenth week?

A 720
B 860
C 880
D 900

Circle your answer

| A | B | C | D |

12 What is the expected total production in units after 15 weeks?

A 9,900
B 10,950
C 11,100
D 11,250

Circle your answer

| A | B | C | D |

Data for questions 13 and 14

A company has received an order for 228,000 units of their product, which will use all available capacity for a number of weeks. Production will be 7,200 units in the first week, 7,400 units in the second week, 7,600 units in the third week, and so on.

13 How many weeks will it take to complete production for the order of 228,000 units?

A 24
B 25
C 26
D 27

Circle your answer

A   B   C   D

14 If the availability of temporary staff is restricted so that after 8 weeks weekly production remains constant at the level achieved in the 8th week, how many weeks, to the nearest week, would it take to complete the order?

A 24
B 25
C 26
D 27

Circle your answer

A   B   C   D

15 Sales of product A in year 1 will be 6,750 units. Thereafter, sales volume will increase by 20% per annum. What will be the sales volume in year 12, to the nearest unit?

A 21,600
B 22,950
C 50,153
D 60,184

Circle your answer

A   B   C   D

16 A geometric progression has a 3rd term of 18 and a common ratio of 3. What is the sum of the first 5 terms of the progression?

A 90
B 242
C 726
D 2,178

Circle your answer

A   B   C   D

Data for questions 17 - 19

The Hart Company Limited have decided to change their mix of sales of two products - Reds and Blues. Sales of Blues are to be gradually reduced to zero and replaced by increased sales of Reds. Blues sold in December amounted to 4,096 units. Sales volume will be halved each month, beginning in January. The first month when only one unit is sold, will be the last month of sales of Blues

1,000 units of Reds will be sold in January, and sales will be increased by 20% per month.

17 How many units of Blues will be sold in total over the period January - September?

A   4,080
B   4,088
C   4,092
D   4,095

Circle your answer

A	B	C	D

18 How many units of Reds will be sold in October next year, to the nearest whole unit?

A   2,800
B   5,160
C   6,192
D   7,430

Circle your answer

A	B	C	D

19 How many units of Reds in total will be sold next year?

A   32,150
B   38,580
C   39,600
D   47,520

Circle your answer

A	B	C	D

Data for questions 20 - 22

A market research team is enquiring into customer purchases of three products - X, Y and Z. 750 housewives have been interviewed and it has been found that each interviewee has at some time purchased either one, two or none of the products. No housewife has purchased all three. The survey shows:

- 177 have purchased product Y only
- 111 have purchased product Z only
- 42 have purchased both products X and Z
- 36 have purchased both products X and Y
- 441 have purchased either X or Y, or both X and Y, but not product Z
- 306 have purchased either Y or Z, or both Y and Z, but not product X

20 How many housewives in the sample have purchased product X only?

A 210
B 228
C 264
D 462

Circle your answer

A   B   C   D

21 How many housewives in the sample have purchased both products Y and Z?

A 18
B 156
C 186
D 288

Circle your answer

A   B   C   D

22 How many housewives in the sample have never purchased products X, Y or Z?

A 138
B 234
C 366
D 384

Circle your answer

A   B   C   D

23 An accountant has used four variables, denoted v, x, y and z, to derive the following equation for monthly cash flow, F:

$$F = 5yz/v(x - 2)$$

Rearranging the terms, what is x equal to?

A   5yz - Fv + 2
B   5yz/v(F-2)
C   5yz/(Fv + 2)
D   (5yz/Fv) + 2

Circle your answer

| A | B | C | D |

Data for questions 24 and 25

A company always makes exactly as many units of its product as it sells. Its fixed costs are £5,000 a year. In addition, it costs £3 to make one unit, and each unit sells for £8.50.

24 At what level of output and sales per year will the company break even (make neither a profit nor a loss)?

A   588 units
B   909 units
C   1,100 units
D   1,700 units

Circle your answer

| A | B | C | D |

25 At what level of output and sales per year will the company make a profit of £8,300 per year?

A   1,157 units
B   1,509 units
C   1,565 units
D   2,418 units

Circle your answer

| A | B | C | D |

26 Two equations containing x and y are as follows:

$$3x - 2y = 30$$
$$4x + 3y = 57.$$

The values of x and y are:

A x = -24, y = 51
B x = 12,   y = 3
C x = 24,   y = 21
D x = 44,   y = 51

Circle your answer

A   B   C   D

27 Two equations are:

$$5y = 3x - 16$$
$$2y = 4x + 2$$

The co-ordinates at which the lines corresponding to these equations intersect are:

A x = -3,   y = -5
B x = 11/7, y = 29/7
C x = 2,   y = 5
D x = 3,   y = 7/5

Circle your answer

A   B   C   D

28 The relationship between quantity demanded and price of a product is known to be linear and of the form:

P   = x + yQ, where
P   = price of product
Q   = quantity demanded in thousands
x,y   = constants

A market research report has shown that quantity demanded will be 17,000 units at a selling price of £14 per unit, and 14,000 units at a selling price of £20 per unit.

The values of x and y are:

A x = -8,   y = 2
B x = -20, y = 2
C x = 24,   y = -½
D x = 48,   y = -2

Circle your answer

A   B   C   D

29 Three equations containing p, q and r are as follows:

$$p + 2q - r = 12$$
$$p + q + 2r = 5$$
$$3p - q + r = 4$$

The values of p and q are:

A   p = ⅓,   q = 6
B   p = 3,   q = ⅓
C   p = 3,   q = 4
D   p = ⅓,   q = 4

Circle your answer

A   B   C   D

30   Given that $(x - 8)(x - 3) = 2 + 2x$, what are the roots of the equation?

A   x = 11   and x = 2
B   x = -11   and x = 2
C   x = 6.5   and x = 4.5
D   x = 6.5   and x = -4.5

Circle your answer

A   B   C   D

31 $3x^2 - 10x - 8$ can be factorised as:

A   (3x - 2)(x + 4)
B   (3x - 4)(x - 2)
C   (3x + 2)(x - 4)
D   (3x + 4)(x - 2)

Circle your answer

A   B   C   D

32   Two equations containing x and y are:

$$x^2 + 5xy + 4y^2 = 55$$
$$x^2 + 7xy + 12y^2 = 99$$

The possible values of x are:

A   x = -88   and x = -22
B   x = -3   and x = 22
C   x = 3   and x = -3
D   x = 3   and x = -22

Circle your answer

A   B   C   D

33   If $y = 3x^2 + 8x - 7$, what values of x would give a value for y of 4?

A   x = -11 and x = 3
B   x = -3⅔ and x = 1
C   x = -3 and x = ⅓
D   x = -1 and x = 3⅔

Circle your answer

A   B   C   D

34 A distribution firm has set a performance target to achieve same-day delivery on 90% of deliveries. 1,500 deliveries have been made so far this month, of which only 88% were same-day. There are 750 deliveries still to be made this month. What percentage of these remaining deliveries must be same-day deliveries, if the performance target is to be met for this month?

A 92%
B 94%
C 96%
D 98%

Circle your answer

A   B   C   D

35 Two equations are as follows:

$$y = 7x - 4$$
$$3x = 2y + 9$$

Which of the following expresses these equations in matrix form?

A $\begin{pmatrix} -7 & 3 \\ 1 & -2 \end{pmatrix} \begin{pmatrix} x \\ y \end{pmatrix} = \begin{pmatrix} -4 \\ 9 \end{pmatrix}$

B $\begin{pmatrix} -7 & 1 \\ 3 & -2 \end{pmatrix} \begin{pmatrix} x \\ y \end{pmatrix} = \begin{pmatrix} 9 \\ -4 \end{pmatrix}$

C $\begin{pmatrix} -7 & 1 \\ 3 & -2 \end{pmatrix} \begin{pmatrix} x \\ y \end{pmatrix} = \begin{pmatrix} -4 \\ 9 \end{pmatrix}$

D $\begin{pmatrix} -7 & 3 \\ 1 & -2 \end{pmatrix} \begin{pmatrix} x \\ y \end{pmatrix} = \begin{pmatrix} 9 \\ -4 \end{pmatrix}$

Circle your answer

A   B   C   D

36 If $P = \begin{pmatrix} 3 & 2 \\ 4 & 7 \end{pmatrix}$ and $Q = \begin{pmatrix} 1 & -3 \\ 0.5 & -2 \end{pmatrix}$,

what is PQ?

A $\begin{pmatrix} 4 & -13 \\ 7.5 & -26 \end{pmatrix}$

B $\begin{pmatrix} -26 & 13 \\ -7.5 & 4 \end{pmatrix}$

C $\begin{pmatrix} 26 & -13 \\ 7.5 & -4 \end{pmatrix}$

D $\begin{pmatrix} 4 & 7.5 \\ -13 & -26 \end{pmatrix}$

Circle your answer

A   B   C   D

19

37 If R = $\begin{pmatrix} 2 & 0 & -3 \\ -1 & 7 & 0 \end{pmatrix}$ and S = $\begin{pmatrix} 1 & 9 \\ 2 & -5 \\ -4 & 3 \end{pmatrix}$,

what is RS?

A $\begin{pmatrix} -44 & -9 \\ -13 & 14 \end{pmatrix}$

B $\begin{pmatrix} 14 & 13 \\ 9 & -44 \end{pmatrix}$

C $\begin{pmatrix} -9 & -14 \\ 44 & -13 \end{pmatrix}$

D $\begin{pmatrix} 14 & 9 \\ 13 & -44 \end{pmatrix}$

Circle your answer

A	B	C	D

38 What is the inverse of $\begin{pmatrix} 4 & 1 \\ 8 & 3 \end{pmatrix}$?

A $\begin{pmatrix} 4 & 8 \\ 1 & 3 \end{pmatrix}$

B $\begin{pmatrix} 0.75 & -0.25 \\ -2 & 1 \end{pmatrix}$

C $\begin{pmatrix} 3 & -1 \\ -8 & 4 \end{pmatrix}$

D $\begin{pmatrix} 0.75 & 0.25 \\ 2 & 1 \end{pmatrix}$

Circle your answer

A	B	C	D

39 which of the following is an identity matrix?

A $\begin{pmatrix} 1 & 0 & 0 \\ 1 & 0 & 0 \\ 1 & 0 & 0 \end{pmatrix}$

B $\begin{pmatrix} 1 & 1 & 1 \\ 0 & 0 & 0 \\ 0 & 0 & 0 \end{pmatrix}$

C $\begin{pmatrix} 1 & 0 & 0 \\ 0 & 1 & 0 \\ 0 & 0 & 1 \end{pmatrix}$

D $\begin{pmatrix} 0 & 0 & 1 \\ 0 & 1 & 0 \\ 1 & 0 & 0 \end{pmatrix}$

Circle your answer

A	B	C	D

40 A company wishes to maximise the monthly profit which it earns from its two products, X and Y. Data concerning the two products are as follows:

Product X has a selling price of £15 and a variable cost of £13 per unit
Product Y has a selling price of £41 and a variable cost of £38 per unit
Company fixed costs are £5,200 per month

Production and sales of the two products are subject to various constraints and the accountant has used the graphical method of linear programming to establish the appropriate product mix. From the graph, the vertices of the feasibility polygon are:

1.	x = 4,000,	y = 0
2.	x = 2,400,	y = 1,200
3.	x = 210,	y = 1,300
4.	x = 0,	y = 1,300

where x, y = production and sales of products X and Y respectively.

What is the maximum achievable monthly profit?

A £3,200
B £4,400
C £8,400
D £9,600

Circle your answer

A   B   C   D

---

41 A company produces two products L and M, such that at least five times as many units of L must be produced as units of M. If L = the number of units of product L produced and M = the number of units of product M produced, then the constraint is written algebraically as:

A   5L ≥ M
B   5M ≥ L
C   L ≥ 5M
D   M ≥ 5L

Circle your answer

A   B   C   D

Data for questions 42 - 44

A company manufactures three products, P, Q and R, using the following labour inputs per unit:

Type of labour	Product P labour hours	Product Q labour hours	Product R labour hours
Unskilled	4	7	2
Semi-skilled	2	6	12
Skilled	6	8	4

Continued...

Production and sales of the products are subject to the following constraints:

(a)   the availability of semi-skilled labour is limited to 7,000 hours per period;

(b)   additional skilled labour can be made available at short notice, and the company wishes to make full use of the 4,000 hours of skilled labour which have already been contracted for next period;

(c)   due to market commitments, at least 20% of the total units output for next period must be product P.

42 Using P, Q and R to represent the production and sales of products P, Q and R respectively, the constraint on semi-skilled labour can be expressed as:

A   P + 3Q + 6R $<$ 3,500
B   2P + 6Q + 12R $>$ 7,000
C   4P + 2Q + 6R $<$ 7,000
D   7P + 3Q + 8R $<$ 7,000

Circle your answer

| A | B | C | D |

43 Using the notation as in the previous question, the constraint on skilled labour can be expressed as:

A   2P + 12Q + 4R $>$ 4,000
B   3P + 4Q + 2R $>$ 2,000
C   4P + 2Q + 6R $<$ 4,000
D   6P + 8Q + 4R $<$ 4,000

Circle your answer

| A | B | C | D |

44 Using the notation as in the previous two questions, the constraint on the proportion of sales of product P can be expressed as:

A   0.8P + Q + R $>$ 0
B   P + 0.8Q + 0.8R $>$ 0
C   P - 0.2Q - 0.2R $>$ 0
D   4P - Q - R $>$ 0

Circle your answer

| A | B | C | D |

45 A production manager is using a graphical linear programme to determine the optimum production mix for two products, E and F. He has established the following two constraints:

$$3E + 4F \leqslant 36$$
$$F \leqslant 2$$

where E, F are the production quantities of products E and F respectively. Which of the following graphs correctly depicts the feasibility polygon for this decision?

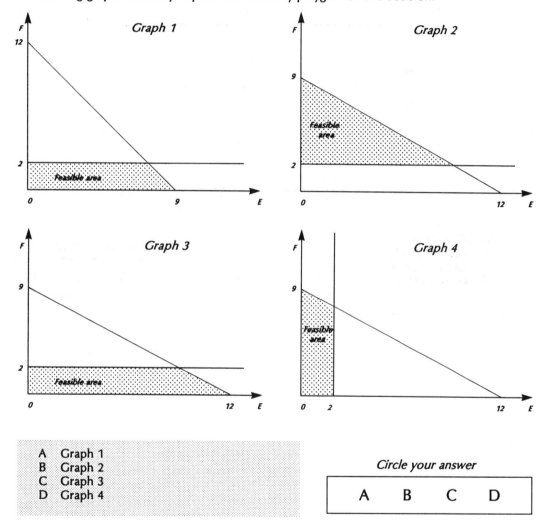

A Graph 1
B Graph 2
C Graph 3
D Graph 4

Circle your answer

A   B   C   D

46 A company wishes to maximise the total contribution from products L and M. The products earn a contribution of £4 per unit and £3 per unit respectively.

Which of the following graph(s) correctly depict(s) an iso-contribution line for the company's objective function?

23

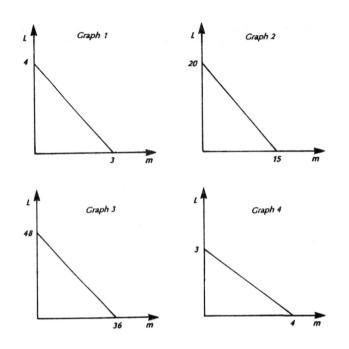

A   Graph 1 only
B   Graphs 1 and 2
C   Graphs 2 and 3
D   Graph 4 only

Circle your answer

A   B   C   D

CHAPTER 2

CALCULUS

This chapter covers the following topics:

- Differentiation
- Maximum and minimum points
- Integration
- Economic order quantity

1. Differentiation

1.1 Differential calculus is a branch of mathematics which is used to calculate the rate of change in one variable with respect to changes in another variable. For example it can be used to estimate:

(a) the rate of change in total revenue as sales volume is increased (this is called the *marginal revenue* at any level of output);

(b) the rate of change in total costs as production volume is increased (this is called the *marginal cost* at any level of output);

(c) the rate of change of a car's maximum speed as the weight of luggage carried is increased.

1.2 The rate of change is found by means of *differentiation*. If we have a function
$$y = ax^n$$

where x is the independent variable and y is the dependent variable, we can find the rate of change in y per unit change in x by differentiating y with respect to x:

If $y = ax^n$, $\dfrac{dy}{dx} = nax^{n-1}$

1.3 Here are some particular points that you should note.

(a) If there are several expressions in the function, each element is differentiated separately.

For example, if $y = 2x^4 - 3x^3 + 6x^2$

$$\frac{dy}{dx} = 4(2)x^3 - 3(3)x^2 + 2(6)x$$
$$= 8x^3 - 9x^2 + 12x$$

(b) On differentiation, any constant disappears. For example, if $y = 3x^2 + 8$, the constant, 8, disappears on differentiation:

$$\frac{dy}{dx} = 2(3)x^{(2-1)} = 6x$$

(c) If the 'power' of x is one, the corresponding value on differentiation is the coefficient of x in the original function. For example, if $y = 5x$

$$\frac{dy}{dx} = 1(5)x^{(1-1)} = 5x^0 = 5 \times 1 = 5$$

(d) The differentiation rule also applies when 'negative powers' are involved.

For example, if $y = \dfrac{3}{x^2}$

$$= 3x^{-2}$$

$$\frac{dy}{dx} = -2(3)x^{(-2-1)}$$

$$= -6x^{-3}$$

$$= \frac{-6}{x^3}$$

1.4 If we have a curve, for example $y = x^2$, the rate of change in y at any value of x is shown by the gradient or slope of the curve at that point. This can be found by differentiating:

$$\frac{dy}{dx} = 2x$$

Thus when $x = 3$, the gradient of the curve is $2 \times 3 = 6$.

A positive gradient slopes up from left to right; a negative gradient slopes down from left to right. A larger positive or negative gradient corresponds to a steeper slope.

2. Maximum and minimum points

2.1 At a 'turning point' in a curve, the gradient will be zero; ie at the point where the gradient changes from positive to negative (a maximum point), or from negative to positive (a minimum point), $\frac{dy}{dx}$ = zero.

2.2 If we have a graph of a function, and have found the gradient of the curve as dy/dx, we can differentiate this again to find the rate at which the *gradient* of the curve is increasing or decreasing. This is called the 'second derivative' of a function and is denoted

$$\frac{d^2y}{dx^2}$$

The second derivative is used to distinguish between maximum and minimum points.

Rules for testing whether a turning point is at a maximum or minimum value.

(a) If $\dfrac{d^2y}{dx^2} > 0$ (is greater than 0, ie is positive) there is a minimum point.

(b) If $\dfrac{d^2y}{dx^2} < 0$ (is less than 0, ie is negative) there is a maximum point.

For example, if $y = x^3 - 5x^2 + 3x - 6$

$$\frac{dy}{dx} = 3x^2 - 10x + 3$$

(1) At a maximum or minimum point, $\dfrac{dy}{dx} = 0$

$$3x^2 - 10x + 3 = 0$$

Factorising,
$$(3x - 1)\ (x - 3) = 0$$
$$x = \tfrac{1}{3} \text{ and } x = 3$$

This tells us that y had a maximum or minimum value when $x = \tfrac{1}{3}$ and when $x = 3$. We must find out whether y has a maximum or minimum value at each of these values for x.

(2) Differentiating $\dfrac{dy}{dx}$: $\dfrac{d^2y}{dx^2} = 6x - 10$

(a) When $x = \tfrac{1}{3}$, $\dfrac{d^2y}{dx^2} = \dfrac{6}{3} - 10 = -8$

This is a negative value, so there is a maximum point when $x = \tfrac{1}{3}$.

(b) When $x = 3$, $\dfrac{d^2y}{dx^2} = 6(3) - 10 = 8$

This is a positive value, so there is a minimum point where $x = 3$.

The curve $y = x^3 - 5x^2 + 3x - 6$ has the following shape, on which we can see the maximum and the minimum

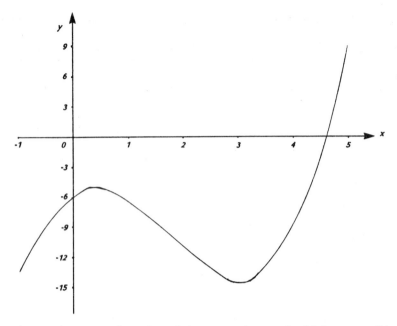

Note that the maximum we have found does not give us the highest possible value of y nor does the minimum we have found give us the lowest possible value of y. We show that the points we have found are only a maximum and a minimum relative to nearby points on the curve by referring to them as a *local maximum* and a *local minimum*.

3. Integration

3.1 Integration, or integral calculus, is the reverse of differentiation.
The *integral* of a function of x, which if differentiated would yield that function f(x), is denoted by:

$$\int f(x)dx$$

3.2 The general formula for integration is:

$$\int ax^b dx = \frac{a}{(b + 1)} x^{b + 1}$$

This reverses the process of differentiation. For example:

$$\int (7x^2 - x^3 + 14)\, dx = \frac{7x^{2+1}}{3} - \frac{1x^{3+1}}{4} + \frac{14x^{0+1}}{1} + c$$

$$= \frac{7x^3}{3} - \frac{x^4}{4} + 14x + c$$

You will notice that we have added c, a constant, at the end of our solution. This is because there could be a constant, which would vanish on differentiation.

3.3 Integral calculus is used to work out the change in the value of y between two given values of x, where f(x) is the rate of change of y as x changes. This would be written as:

$$\int_a^b f(x)dx \quad \text{where a and b are two given values of x.}$$

For example, suppose we want to find the change in total production cost per hour (y) when output (q) is increased from 5 units to 8 units per hour. If *marginal* production cost is given by $\frac{dy}{dq} = 3 + 2q$, we could solve this problem as follows.

We want to find: $\int_5^8 (3 + 2q)\, dq$

Integrating, we get $\left[3q + q^2 + c \right]_5^8$

When q = 8, total costs will be $3(8) + (8)^2 + c =$ £88 + c $\left.\begin{array}{c}\\\\\end{array}\right\}$ the c vanishes in the
When q = 5, total costs will be $3(5) + (5)^2 + c =$ £40 + c subtraction

The increase in cost is therefore   £48

4. Economic order quantity

4.1 The economic order quantity (EOQ) or economic batch quantity (EBQ) is the optimal ordering quantity for an item of stock which will minimise the total costs of storing and ordering.

4.2 The total cost per period of ordering and holding stock is $\dfrac{Qh}{2} + \dfrac{cd}{Q}$

where   Q = quantity per order
        h = cost of holding one unit in stock for one period
        c = cost of placing one order
        d = total demand in units per period

29

4.3 The EOQ formula is derived using differential calculus, and is as follows:

$$EOQ = \sqrt{\frac{2cd}{h}}$$

4.4 If a company manufactures its own requirements of a stock item, then c, the cost of placing an order, can be replaced by the cost of setting up the machine for production. The resulting calculation is usually referred to as the Economic Batch Quantity. However, this simple substitution of terms only applies if production is instantaneous, ie the time required for a production run is nil.

4.5 If re-supply of stock is gradual, the formula needs to be adapted to allow for the fact that stock replenishment is occurring gradually at the same time as stock is being gradually consumed:

$$EBQ \text{ (gradual replenishment)} = \sqrt{\frac{2cd}{h(1- d/r)}}$$

Where c = set up cost per batch
       d = demand in the period
       h = holding cost per unit of stock per period
       r = production rate per period (ie quantity which would be produced by continuous production throughout the period)

QUESTIONS

1 If $y = 4x^3 + 2x^2 + 7x - 9$, what is the value of $\frac{dy}{dx}$ when x = 4?

A   206
B   215
C   236
D   307

Circle your answer

A   B   C   D

2 What is the gradient of the curve $y = 7x^2 + x - 6$, at the point where x = -3?

A   -41
B   -43
C   -45
D   -47

Circle your answer

A   B   C   D

3 If $2s = 3t^2 - 4t + 6$, what is the value of $\frac{ds}{dt}$ when t = 5?

A   13
B   16
C   26
D   32

Circle your answer

A   B   C   D

4 If $y = \frac{14}{x} - \frac{2}{x^2}$, then $\frac{dy}{dx}$ is equal to

A $14 - \frac{4}{x}$

B $\frac{14}{x^2} - \frac{4}{x^3}$

C $-\frac{14}{x^2} + \frac{4}{x^3}$

D $-\frac{28}{x^2} + \frac{4}{x^3}$

Circle your answer

A   B   C   D

5 If $p = \sqrt{q} - \dfrac{1}{q} + \dfrac{q}{2}$, what is the value of $\dfrac{dp}{dq}$ when $q = 4$?

A $\dfrac{3}{16}$

B $\dfrac{11}{16}$

C $\dfrac{13}{16}$

D $\dfrac{5}{4}$

Circle your answer

A   B   C   D

6 If $u = 4\sqrt{v} - \dfrac{1}{v^3}$ then $\dfrac{du}{dv}$ equals

A $\dfrac{2}{\sqrt{v}} + \dfrac{3}{v^2}$

B $\dfrac{2}{\sqrt{v}} + \dfrac{3}{v^4}$

C $\dfrac{2}{\sqrt{v}} - \dfrac{3}{v^4}$

D $-\dfrac{1}{\sqrt{v}} - \dfrac{6}{v^2}$

Circle your answer

A   B   C   D

7 The total costs of manufacturing a product are given by:

$$£C = 16 + Q + 3Q^2$$

where $£C$ = total cost
         Q = volume of production

What is the marginal cost when the volume of production is 8 units?

A   £49
B   £56
C   £72
D   £216

Circle your answer

A   B   C   D

8 A company has estimated that the demand curve for its product is P = 8 - 0.05Q, where P is the unit price and Q is the quantity of sales, in thousands. The total cost function is C = 400 + 5Q + 0.1Q^2 . (C is in thousands of pounds).

Economic theory states that profit is maximised when marginal cost is equal to marginal revenue. Applying this theory, what quantity of sales will maximise the profit?

A   2,500 units
B   10,000 units
C   12,000 units
D   30,000 units

Circle your answer

A   B   C   D

9 The average unit cost of a product is given by c = 3v^2 - 180v + 4,000 where c is the average unit cost and v is the volume of production. At what volume of production will average unit cost be lowest?

A   30 units
B   40 units
C   60 units
D   70 units

Circle your answer

A   B   C   D

10 The demand for a product is given by D = 35p + 7,000 - 7p^2 , where D is the annual demand and p is the price per unit. Which of the following functions of price will equal zero at maximum total revenue (D x p)?

A   35p + 7,000 - 7p^2
B   70 - 42p
C   70p + 7,000 - 21p^2
D   35 - 14p

Circle your answer

A   B   C   D

11 If y = 210x - 5x^2 , which of the following statements is/are true?

Statement
1.   y is at a maximum when x = 21
2.   y is at a minimum when x = 21
3.   The graph of y cuts the x axis at one point only, when x = 21
4.   The graph of y cuts the x axis at one point only, when x = 42

A   Statement 1 only
B   Statement 2 only
C   Statements 2 and 3 only
D   Statements 1 and 4 only

Circle your answer

A   B   C   D

12 If $y = x^3 - 9x^2 + 24x - 4$, which of the following statements are true?

Statement
1. y is at a maximum when x = 2
2. y is at a maximum when x = 4
3. y is at a minimum when x = 2
4. y is at a minimum when x = 4

A   Statements 1 and 2 only
B   Statements 1 and 4 only
C   Statements 2 and 3 only
D   Statements 3 and 4 only

Circle your answer

A	B	C	D

13 $y = x^3 - 4x^2 - 11x + 6$

For what value of x will y be at a minimum?

A   -1
B   -3
C $3\frac{2}{3}$
D   11

Circle your answer

A	B	C	D

Data for questions 14 - 16

A company has established the following functions to represent the costs and revenue for its product.

$$c = q^2 - 1.25q + 30$$
$$r = 6.5q^2 - q^3 + 10q \text{ (applies up to q = 7)}$$

where   £c = total cost
q = quantity produced and sold, in thousands
£r = total revenue

14 At what volume of output would total revenue be maximised?

A   667 units
B   3,333 units
C   5,000 units
D   6,667 units

Circle your answer

A	B	C	D

15 What would be the marginal cost at an output of 4,800 units?

A £8.35
B £10.85
C £38.35
D £40.00

Circle your answer

A   B   C   D

16 At what volume of output would profit be maximised?

A 833 units
B 4,500 units
C 6,533 units
D 13,500 units

Circle your answer

A   B   C   D

17 $\int_{0}^{2} 3x^3 \, dx$ equals

A 12
B 24
C 36
D 48

Circle your answer

A   B   C   D

18 $\int_{0}^{3} (6q^2 + 4q - 7) \, dq$ equals

A 40
B 51
C 59
D 72

Circle your answer

A   B   C   D

19 $\int_{3}^{6} (4q - 1) \, dq$ equals

A 4
B 5.5
C 12
D 51

Circle your answer

A   B   C   D

20 $\int_{1}^{2} (3v - \frac{2}{v^2} + 0.25)\, dv$ is equal to

   A 3.75
   B 4.5
   C 7.0
   D 7.5

Circle your answer

A	B	C	D

21 The marginal cost of manufacturing a unit of product P is $7 + 0.04q$, where q represents the volume of production. By how much will total cost increase when output is increased from 300 units to 400 units?

   A £1,100
   B £2,100
   C £9,900
   D £14,700

Circle your answer

A	B	C	D

Data for questions 22 and 23

A company manufactures a single product for which the following marginal cost and marginal revenue functions have been derived:

      Marginal cost, £MC   = $1 + q$
      Marginal revenue, £MR = $80 - 0.5q$

where q is the quantity of product manufactured and sold.

The company holds no stocks, and is currently manufacturing 12 units per day. They are considering increasing output to 16 units per day, which would have no effect on their cost and revenue structures.

22 By how much will total daily revenue increase, if output is increased to 16 units per day?

   A £78
   B £208
   C £264
   D £292

Circle your answer

A	B	C	D

23 By how much will total daily profit increase, if output is increased to 16 units per day?

A £60
B £74
C £204
D £232

Circle your answer

A   B   C   D

24 A company uses 4,225 units of a stock item each year, at a constant rate. It costs £5 to place an order for the item, and £0.10 to hold one unit in stock for a year.

What is the Economic Order Quantity in units?

A 10
B 13
C 460
D 650

Circle your answer

A   B   C   D

25 The demand for a component occurs at a steady rate and amounts to 45,000 units each year. It costs £20 to place an order with component suppliers and 15 pence to store a unit for one calendar month. What is the order quantity to minimise the total costs of ordering and storing the components?

A 90
B 100
C 1,000
D 3,464

Circle your answer

A   B   C   D

26 A company manufactures its own components for stock at the rate of 1,000 units per week. Demand for the component is constant at the rate of 400 units per week. It costs £75 to set up the mechanism for each production run and the cost of storing a stock item is £0.10 per week. What is the economic batch quantity, to the nearest unit, to minimise the total costs of setting up the machines and storing the components?

A 775
B 1,000
C 1,225
D 1,581

Circle your answer

A   B   C   D

27 At the economic order quantity, the ratio of annual stockholding costs to annual ordering costs is

A h:c
B 1:1
C c:h
D 2:1

Circle your answer

A   B   C   D

CHAPTER 3

SIMPLE AND COMPOUND INTEREST. DISCOUNTING

This chapter covers the following topics:

- Simple interest
- Compound interest
- Annual percentage rate (APR)
- Discounting
- Net present value
- Annuities
- Internal rate of return

1. Simple interest

1.1 If you invest money, and get simple interest on it, each year you will earn a percentage of your original investment. Thus if you invested £1,000 at 8%, the interest each year would be £80.

> *Simple interest formula:* $\quad S_n = P + nrP$
>
> where $\quad S_n$ = sum invested after n periods
> $\quad\quad\quad P$ = original sum invested (the principal)
> $\quad\quad\quad r$ = interest rate
> $\quad\quad\quad n$ = number of periods

2. Compound interest

2.1 Compound interest is far more common than simple interest. Bank deposit accounts and building society accounts pay compound interest. The interest earned is credited to the account and future interest payments are based on the original investment plus interest previously credited. Thus at 10%, £1,000 earns £100 interest in a year. In the next year, £1,100 earns interest of £1,100 x 10% = £110, and the investment will have grown to £1,100 + £110 = £1,210.

> *Compound interest formula:* $\quad S_n = P(1 + r)^n$
>
> where $\quad S_n$ = sum invested after n periods
> $\quad\quad\quad P$ = original sum invested (the principal)
> $\quad\quad\quad r$ = interest rate
> $\quad\quad\quad n$ = number of periods

2.2 Investors often make regular savings. For example, suppose that a person invests £400 now, and a further £400 at the start of each year for 2 more years. Interest is earned at 10% per annum. He may want to work out what the total investment will amount to 3 years from now.

(a) Using $S_n = P(1 + r)^n$

			£
(Year 0)	The first year's investment will grow in value to	$£400(1.10)^3$ =	532.40
(Year 1)	The second year's investment will grow in value to	$£400(1.10)^2$ =	484.00
(Year 2)	The third year's investment will grow in value to	$£400(1.10)^1$ =	440.00
	Value of investment after three years		£1,456.40

We have a geometric progression here. We want the sum

$$400(1.1) + 400(1.1)^2 + 400(1.1)^3$$

(b) Using the geometric progression formula, $S_n = \dfrac{a(1 - r^n)}{(1 - r)}$

the value of the investment after three years $= \dfrac{£400\,(1.1)(1-(1.1)^3\,)}{(1 - 1.1)}$

$= £1,456.40.$

It is important, when dealing with investment calculations that involve regular savings, to check (1) when the first instalment is made - now or at the end of period 1 and (2) when the final instalment is made, and whether this has any time to earn interest.

3. Annual percentage rate (APR)

3.1 If interest rates are quoted in terms of a short time period, for instance a month, they can be converted to the equivalent annual percentage rate (APR). Credit card companies, for example, may quote a rate of 2% a month, which corresponds to an APR of 26.8%.

	APR	=	$(1 + r)^t - 1$
where	r	=	rate of interest charged over the shorter time period
	t	=	number of times interest is charged in a year

For example, if interest is charged at 3% per month compound:

APR $= (1 + 0.03)^{12} - 1$
$= 0.426$

The equivalent annual percentage rate is 42.6%.

3.2 Quite often, the annual rate of interest quoted to investors is a so-called 'nominal' rate of interest. For example, a building society may offer investors 10% per annum interest payable half-yearly. If the 10% is a nominal rate of interest, the building society would in fact pay 5% every 6 months, compounded, so that the true annual rate of interest would be:

$(1.05)^2 - 1 = 0.1025$ or 10.25% per annum.

4. Discounting

4.1 Discounting is the reverse of compounding. If we wish to have £1 in n years' time, how much money do we need to invest *now* at an interest rate of r% in order to obtain the required sum of money in the future?

> The discounting formula is $P = \dfrac{S_n}{(1 + r)^n}$
>
> where P is the 'present value' of a future sum of money, S_n.

4.2 The term 'present value' is often met in discounted cash flow, and it simply means the amount of money which must be invested now at r% so as to have a future sum of money at the end of year n.

4.3 For example, if the interest rate is 10% the present value (PV) of £1 to be received in year 2 (ie 2 years from now)

$$= £1 \times \frac{1}{(1.10)^2}$$

$$= £1 \times 0.83 = £0.83$$

The value 0.83 could also be found against year 2 in the 10% column on a table of present value factors. These tables are also called discount factor tables. They are given at the end of this book, and you can look up numbers in them to save working them out.

Similarly, using the same column, the present value of £800 to be received in year 9 is equal to £800 x 0.42 = £336. Thus if the interest rate is 10%, you could invest £336 now and have £800 nine years from now. Being given £336 today is as good as being given £800 nine years hence.

5. Net present value

5.1 Net present value (NPV) can be used as a basis for appraising capital expenditure proposals. The NPV is the value obtained by discounting all cash flows to their present value, and then adding together the discounted values.

Example: A company is considering an investment of £18,000. The cash inflows from the investment will be £10,000 at the end of year 1 and £14,000 at the end of year 2. The company requires a return of 10% per annum.

Year	Cash flow	Discount factor at 10% (from tables)	Present value
	£		£
0	(18,000)	1.00	(18,000)
1	10,000	0.91	9,100
2	14,000	0.83	11,620
		Net present value	2,720

Because the NPV is positive, the investment is worthwhile. The investment is as good as being given £2,720 today, and of course one would accept such a gift. If the NPV had been (say) - £1,000, making the investment would have been as bad as giving away £1,000 today, so we would not make the investment.

6. Annuities

6.1 An annuity is a constant cash flow occurring each year for a given number of years. To calculate the present value of a constant annual cash flow, or annuity, we can multiply the annual cash flow by the sum of the discount factors for the relevant years. This total is a 'cumulative present value' factor or 'annuity' factor. As with annual present value factors, there are tables (at the end of this book) which show the cumulative factors. For example, the cumulative present value factor for 5 years at 11% per annum is 3.70. Note that the table factors assume that the first instalment is received one year from now.

6.2 One use of annuity factors is to calculate the annual repayments on a loan or mortgage. Since the present value of an annuity, A, is:

PV = A x annuity factor from the tables

$$A = \frac{PV(amount\ of\ loan)}{annuity\ factor}$$

For example, if a £50,000 mortgage at 14% per annum is to be repaid in fifteen annual instalments:

$$Annual\ repayment = \frac{£50,000}{PV\ factor\ of\ £1\ per\ annum\ at\ 14\%\ for\ 15\ years}$$

$$= \frac{£50,000}{6.14} = £8,143$$

6.3 One other value that you should know how to calculate is the present value of an annuity which will be received or paid for ever (in perpetuity), the first receipt or payment being one year from now.

Present value of a perpetuity $= \dfrac{a}{r}$ where a = amount per year   r = interest rate

42

7. Internal rate of return

7.1 The internal rate of return (IRR) on a series of cash inflows and outflows is the discount rate at which the net present value is zero.

7.2 For annuities, the IRR can be found with tables. If, for example, a payment of £8,000 will secure an annuity of £1,061 for 12 years, we have:

$$£1,061 \times \text{annuity factor} = £8,000$$
$$\text{annuity factor} = 8,000/1,061 = 7.54$$

Reading along the twelve year row in annuity tables, we find 7.54 under 8%, so this must be the internal rate of return.

7.3 Where cash flows are uneven, we can get a good approximation to the IRR by finding the net present value at two discount rates, and then interpolating.

If a = one interest rate
    b = the other interest rate
    A is the NPV at rate a
    B is the NPV at rate b

then the approximate IRR is

$$a + \frac{A}{A - B} (b - a)$$

For example, if a stream of cash flows had a net present value of £2,000 at 10% and a net present value of - £580 at 20%, the approximate IRR would be

$$10 + \frac{2,000}{2,000 - -580} (20 - 10) = 17.75\%.$$

QUESTIONS

1 How much will an investor have after 8 years if he invests £2,000 at 12% per annum simple interest?

A £1,920
B £3,680
C £3,920
D £4,952

Circle your answer

A   B   C   D

2 How much simple interest would be earned on an investment of £1,200 at 14.4% per annum for 10 years?

A £1,728
B £2,928
C £3,407
D £4,607

Circle your answer

A   B   C   D

3 How much simple interest would be earned on an investment of £700 at 2% per month over 3 years?

A £42
B £504
C £728
D £1,204

Circle your answer

A   B   C   D

4 In four years an investment of £900 has grown to £1,548. What has been the monthly rate of simple interest?

A 1.1%
B 1.5%
C 15%
D 18%

Circle your answer

A   B   C   D

Please answer questions 5 - 20 using interest and discount factors worked out on your calculator, rather than looking up factors in tables. If your calculator has a button for interest factors, please do not use it.

5 What would be the value after 4 years, to the nearest £, of an investment of £2,250 earning a compound interest rate of 16% per annum?

A £2,397
B £3,512
C £3,690
D £4,074

Circle your answer

A   B   C   D

6 How much compound interest would be earned if £1,350 was invested at 12% for 6 years, to the nearest £1?

A £972
B £1,092
C £1,315
D £2,665

Circle your answer

A   B   C   D

7 A sum of money invested at compound interest of 11% per annum has grown to £23,914 after 10 years. What was the original sum invested, to the nearest £1?

A £8,382
B £8,422
C £9,220
D £11,388

Circle your answer

A   B   C   D

8 After 15 years an investment of £600 has grown to £6,740. What annual rate of compound interest has been applied?

A 6.82%
B 11.75%
C 17.50%
D 18.86%

Circle your answer

A   B   C   D

9 The manager of a pension fund has set a target of 53% growth in the value of the fund after 4 years. The annual compound percentage growth rate (to 2 decimal places) is equivalent to

A   8.88%
B   11.22%
C   13.25%
D   15.23%

Circle your answer

A   B   C   D

10 £2,500 invested on 1 January 1975 had grown to be worth £61,482 on 31 December 1989. The equivalent annual compound growth rate (to 2 decimal places) is

A   23.80%
B   25.70%
C   57.29%
D   63.95%

Circle your answer

A   B   C   D

11 An investor places £8,000 into an investment for 10 years. The compound rate of interest earned is 8% for the first 4 years and 12% for the last 6 years. At the end of the 10 years the investment (to the nearest £) is worth

A   £16,320
B   £21,483
C   £21,517
D   £26,854

Circle your answer

A   B   C   D

12 Walter invested £5,000 in a bank deposit account which pays interest of 9% per annum, added to the account at the end of each year. He made one withdrawal of £1,500 at the end of 3 years. What was the balance in the account at the end of 5 years, to the nearest £?

A   £5,285
B   £5,911
C   £6,193
D   £6,399

Circle your answer

A   B   C   D

13 An item of equipment currently costs £4,000. The rate of inflation for the next 3 years is expected to be 8% per annum, then 10% per annum for the following 2 years. The price of the equipment is expected to increase in line with inflation. The price, to the nearest £, after 5 years will be

A   £5,760
B   £5,800
C   £6,097
D   £6,155

Circle your answer

A   B   C   D

14 A credit card company charges its customers compound interest at the rate of 2.25% per month. The equivalent annual percentage rate, to 1 decimal place, is

A 27.0%
B 27.7%
C 30.6%
D 34.5%

Circle your answer

A   B   C   D

15 A bank offers depositors a nominal interest rate of 10% per annum, with interest added to their accounts quarterly. The effective annual percentage rate, to 1 decimal place, is

A 8.2%
B 8.3%
C 10.4%
D 11.0%

Circle your answer

A   B   C   D

16 Rita invests £700 on 1 January each year, starting in 1990. Compound interest of 10% is credited on 31 December each year. To the nearest £, the value of her investment on 31 December 1999 will be

A £10,456
B £11,156
C £12.272
D £12,972

Circle your answer

A   B   C   D

17 You will receive £5,000 six years from now. What is the present value at a discount rate of 8%?

A £2,600
B £3,137
C £3,151
D £3,800

Circle your answer

A   B   C   D

18 An investment would involve spending £10,000 now, and getting cash returns of £6,000 one year from now and £8,000 four years from now. What is the net present value of this investment at a discount rate of 10%?

A £919
B £2,732
C £3,151
D £3,636

Circle your answer

A   B   C   D

19 A company uses a discount rate of 14% per annum. What is the present value of an £18,000 cash inflow to be received 4 years from now?

A   £18,000 [1.14 + 1.14^2 + 1.14^3 + 1.14^4]

B $\dfrac{£18,000}{4 \times 1.14}$

C $\dfrac{£18,000}{(1.14)^4}$

D   £18,000 (1.14)^4

Circle your answer

A	B	C	D

20 Mr Jay wishes to invest a lump sum at 12% interest per annum. How much should he invest now in order to have £60,000 at the end of three years?

A   £60,000 - (3 x 0.12 x £60,000)

B   £60,000 $\left[\dfrac{1}{1.12} + \dfrac{1}{1.12^2} + \dfrac{1}{1.12^3} \right]$

C $\dfrac{£60,000}{3 \times 1.12}$

D $\dfrac{£60,000}{(1.12)^3}$

Circle your answer

A	B	C	D

Please answer questions 21 onwards using the tables of discount factors provided at the end of this book.

21 Ravinder wishes to invest a lump sum at 10% interest per annum. How much does he need to invest now if he wishes to withdraw £8,000 at the end of year 2, and to have a remaining balance of £6,000 invested at the end of year 5?

A   £9,400
B   £10,360
C   £24,360
D   £36,660

Circle your answer

A	B	C	D

22 What is the present value of £1,400 earned at the end of each year for 8 years, when the discount rate is 11% per annum?

A £5,810
B £6,600
C £7,210
D £9,975

Circle your answer

A   B   C   D

23 An investment will generate cash flows of £1,800 each year in years 3 to 7 (ie first amount to be received 3 years from now). The discount rate is 15% per annum. What is the present value of the cash flows?

A £3,377
B £4,554
C £5,930
D £6,830

Circle your answer

A   B   C   D

24 A company is considering a project which will cost £3,400 now and will earn £2,000 per annum in years 1 to 3 (ie first earnings one year from now), and £2,200 per annum in years 4 to 8. The discount rate is 13%. What is the net present value of the project?

A £5,346
B £6,688
C £8,746
D £10,088

Circle your answer

A   B   C   D

25 A company is currently evaluating a project which requires investments of £5,000 now, and £2,000 at the end of year 1. The cash inflows from the project will be £7,000 at the end of year 2 and £6,000 at the end of year 3. If the discount rate is 16%, what is the net present value of the project?

A £2,020
B £2,300
C £3,840
D £5,740

Circle your answer

A   B   C   D

26 A bank has granted a £12,000 loan at 14% interest per annum. The borrower is to repay the loan in 8 equal annual instalments, starting one year from now. To the nearest £, how much must she repay each year?

A £1,710
B £2,586
C £3,180
D £6,960

Circle your answer

A   B   C   D

27 A building society offers a low-start mortgage of £40,000 with 10 annual repayments starting one year from the loan being taken out. The interest rate applying throughout will be 11% per annum, but the repayments will be only £5,000 per annum for the first 5 years. To the nearest £, what equal annual repayments will be required in each of the last 5 years of the mortgage?

A £5,815
B £7,710
C £9,817
D £11,810

Circle your answer

A B C D

28 A company has borrowed from a bank at an interest rate of 13% per annum. The loan must be repaid in 6 equal annual instalments of £12,000, starting one year after the loan was taken out. The amount of the loan is therefore

A £48,000
B £56,200
C £62,900
D £72,400

Circle your answer

A B C D

29 A company is considering a project which would cost £13,000 now and would yield £2,100 per annum in perpetuity, starting one year from now. The cost of capital is 14%. What is the net present value of the project?

A £2,000
B £2,800
C £8,000
D £15,000

Circle your answer

A B C D

30 A payment of £3,000 now will secure receipts of £709 a year for six years, starting one year from now. What is the internal rate of return of this investment?

A 10%
B 11%
C 12%
D 13%

Circle your answer

A B C D

31 A payment of £5,000 now will secure receipts of £804 a year for eleven years, starting *now*. What is the internal rate of return of this investment?

A 11%
B 12%
C 13%
D 14%

Circle your answer

A   B   C   D

32 If a payment of £3,750 now will secure a perpetuity of £514 a year, starting one year from now, what is the internal rate of return of this investment?

A 10.75%
B 12.23%
C 13.71%
D 15.19%

Circle your answer

A   B   C   D

33 An investment has a net present value of £4,000 at 10% and one of -£2,000 at 15%. What is the approximate internal rate of return?

A 11.67%
B 12%
C 13.33%
D 14%

Circle your answer

A   B   C   D

34 An investment of £10,000 now would yield income of £6,000 one year hence and £8,000 three years hence. Using discount rates of 10% and 20%, what is the approximate internal rate of return?

A 12%
B 14%
C 16%
D 18%

Circle your answer

A   B   C   D

CHAPTER 4

DEPRECIATION. TRADE AND SETTLEMENT DISCOUNTS

This chapter covers the following topics:

- Straight line depreciation
- Sum of the digits depreciation
- Reducing balance depreciation
- Sinking funds
- Trade and settlement discounts

1. Straight line depreciation

1.1 Depreciation is an accounting technique whereby the cost of a capital asset is spread over a number of accounting periods. A charge for depreciation is made against the profit for each period, throughout the useful life of the asset. The depreciation charge is often referred to as a 'provision' for depreciation.

1.2 The most common basis for calculating depreciation is the straight line method. By this method, the amount to be depreciated is spread evenly over the life of an asset, so that there is an equal charge in each accounting period.

Annual depreciation charge using the straight line method	=	(Original asset cost - Estimated residual value) Number of years useful life

1.3 The net book value of an asset at the end of an accounting period is equal to the original asset cost *less* the depreciation provided to date.

1.4 Depreciation of leases of land and buildings is usually called *amortisation*. The straight line method is nearly always used for leases.

2. Sum of the digits depreciation

2.1 With this method of depreciation the amount of the charge changes each year. A higher charge is made in earlier years and a lower charge is made in later years, using a system of 'weighting', based on the number of years the asset is expected to last.

2.2 If an asset cost £12,000 and will have no residual value at the end of its five year life, the depreciation is calculated as follows:

Sum of the years' digits = 5 + 4 + 3 + 2 + 1 = 15

∴ Depreciation cost per digit = $\frac{£12,000}{15}$ = £800

Year	Weighting (digits)		Depreciation
			£
1st	5	(5 x 800)	4,000
2nd	4	(4 x 800)	3,200
3rd	3	(3 x 800)	2,400
4th	2	(2 x 800)	1,600
5th	1	(1 x 800)	800
	15		12,000

3. Reducing balance depreciation

3.1 With the reducing balance method, the annual depreciation charge is a constant percentage of the net book value of the asset at the beginning of the year. For example, if an asset is purchased for £10,000 and is to be depreciated by 40% per annum, the depreciation is calculated as follows:

	£
Initial cost	10,000
Year 1 depreciation 40%	(4,000)
Net book value at the end of year 1	6,000
Year 2 depreciation 40%	(2,400)
Net book value at the end of year 2	3,600
Year 3 depreciation 40%	(1,440)
Net book value at the end of year 3	2,160
... and so on	

3.2 To demonstrate the formula used to calculate the percentage rate of annual depreciation, we will use the example in paragraph 3.1:

	Net book value	
Year 1	£6,000	= £10,000 x (1-0.4)
Year 2	£3,600	= £10,000 x $(1-0.4)^2$
Year 3	£2,160	= £10,000 x $(1-0.4)^3$

Net book value of asset at the end of year n = $A(1-r)^n$

where   A is the original cost of the asset
        r is the rate of depreciation as a proportion

This formula enables us to calculate r, given the residual value of the asset, which should be its net book value at the end of its n years of life.

4. Sinking funds

4.1 A sinking fund is an investment into which equal annual instalments are paid, in order to earn sufficient interest so that after a number of years the accumulated investment, including the interest earned, is large enough to pay off a known future commitment.

4.2 In the context of depreciation the known future commitment is the need to replace an asset at the end of its useful life. To ensure that the money is available to buy a replacement, a company might decide to invest cash in a sinking fund during the course of life of the existing asset. Compound interest computations, as covered in chapter 3, can be applied to determine the required annual investments at a given rate of interest.

5. Trade and settlement discounts

5.1 When a sale is made to a customer, there are two main types of discount which may be granted - a trade discount and/or a settlement discount. The type of discount given will depend on the customer and on the terms of the sale.

5.2 A trade discount is a reduction in the cost of goods resulting from the nature of the transaction. It often results from buying goods in bulk on a single purchase, or an important customer might be offered a discount on all purchases, because the total volume of his purchases over time is so large. The discount is usually quoted as a percentage of the invoiced value of goods.

5.3 A settlement discount (also called a cash discount) is a reduction in the amount payable to a supplier, in return for quick payment.

5.4 A single customer can be entitled to both trade discount and settlement discount. If this is so, the settlement discount is calculated on the invoice value *net* of the trade discount.

Example: A customer is entitled to a 5% trade discount and a 1% settlement discount on purchases which have an invoice value of £10,000.

		£
	Invoice value	10,000
less	5% trade discount	(500)
	Net invoice value	9,500
less	1% settlement discount	(95)
	Amount due if payment made early enough to qualify for the settlement discount	9,405

QUESTIONS

1 A packing machine cost £16,000 and is expected to have a useful life of eight years, after which it will be sold for £1,000. Using the straight line method, the annual charge for depreciation will be

- A £1,875
- B £2,000
- C £2,125
- D £2,285

Circle your answer

A   B   C   D

2 A company makes an annual provision of £3,700 for the amortisation of a lease which it purchased five years ago. The lease will expire after a further fifteen years have elapsed. What was the purchase price of the lease?

- A £37,000
- B £55,000
- C £74,000
- D £92,500

Circle your answer

A   B   C   D

3 Pringle Limited have just purchased a 15 year lease for £36,000. They intend to use the lease for 10 years, after which time they expect to be able to sell the remaining term for £6,000. What annual charge for amortisation should be made in the company's accounts?

- A £2,000
- B £2,800
- C £3,000
- D £4,200

Circle your answer

A   B   C   D

4 A delivery vehicle cost £15,000 and has an expected useful life of 4 years, after which it will be sold for £1,000. Using the straight line method of depreciation, what will be the net book value of the vehicle after three years?

- A £3,500
- B £3,750
- C £4,000
- D £4,500

Circle your answer

A   B   C   D

Data for questions 5 - 7

A company uses the sum of the digits method to depreciate its assets. A particular asset has an expected life of 20 years, after which it will have a residual value of £10,500. The original cost of the asset was £73,500.

5 What depreciation charge will be shown in the management accounts for this asset for the first year of its life?

A   £300
B   £3,150
C   £6,000
D   £7,000

Circle your answer

A   B   C   D

6 What would be the depreciation charge in the twelfth year?

A   £2,400
B   £2,700
C   £3,150
D   £3,600

Circle your answer

A   B   C   D

7 The net book value of the asset at the end of the third year will be

A   £45,900
B   £56,400
C   £64,050
D   £71,700

Circle your answer

A   B   C   D

8 An asset which cost £14,000 is to be depreciated by the reducing balance method at the rate of 20% per annum. What will be the depreciation charge in year 3?

A   £112
B   £1,434
C   £1,792
D   £2,800

Circle your answer

A   B   C   D

9 An asset costing £22,000 is to be depreciated using the reducing balance method at a rate of 25% per annum. To the nearest £, what will be the total amount of depreciation charged in the first four years?

A £2,320
B £12,719
C £15,039
D £22,000

Circle your answer

A   B   C   D

Data for questions 10 - 12

A machine cost £18,000 and it is to be depreciated by 15% per annum, on a reducing balance basis.

10 What will be the depreciation charge in year 6?

A £1,018
B £1,198
C £1,409
D £2,700

Circle your answer

A   B   C   D

11 What will be the total amount of depreciation charged in the first five years?

A £7,987
B £8,604
C £10,013
D £13,500

Circle your answer

A   B   C   D

12 To the nearest £, what will be the net book value after eight years?

A £3,600
B £4,905
C £5,770
D £13,095

Circle your answer

A   B   C   D

13 An asset cost £25,000 and at the end of its useful life of 6 years, it is expected to have a residual value of £1,500. To the nearest whole number, what will be the annual percentage rate of depreciation, using the reducing balance method?

A   13%
B   14%
C   37%
D   63%

Circle your answer

A   B   C   D

14 A vehicle is being depreciated on a reducing balance basis, using an annual percentage rate of 18%. If the vehicle originally cost £34,000 and has an estimated useful life of 8 years then the residual value, to the nearest £, is forecast to be

A   £3,747
B   £6,120
C   £6,950
D   £8,476

Circle your answer

A   B   C   D

Data for questions 15 - 17

A set of office furniture cost £10,000 and is expected to have a residual value of £1,000 at the end of its useful life of six years. The furniture is to be depreciated using the reducing balance method.

15 What will be the annual percentage rate of depreciation?

A   15%
B   17%
C   32%
D   68%

Circle your answer

A   B   C   D

16 To the nearest £, what is the depreciation charge for the third year?

A   £696
B   £1,480
C   £1,500
D   £3,200

Circle your answer

A   B   C   D

17 To the nearest £, what will be the net book value at the end of the fifth year?

A £1,454
B £1,667
C £2,138
D £2,500

Circle your answer

A   B   C   D

18 A company wishes to replace a machine in five years' time at an estimated cost of £24,000. The company can earn interest of 15% per annum on money invested in a fund. To the nearest £, how much must be invested at the end of each of the five years in order to have sufficient funds to replace the machine?

A £3,560
B £4,080
C £4,806
D £5,520

Circle your answer

A   B   C   D

19 A removals company intends to set up a reserve fund to enable them to replace a vehicle for £17,000 in two years time. A fixed sum of money will be invested at the end of each six month period, starting six months from now. The nominal annual interest rate will be 10%, compounded every six months. To the nearest £, how much should be invested each period?

A £3,663
B £3,756
C £3,825
D £3,944

Circle your answer

A   B   C   D

20 A squash club wishes to set up a reserve fund so that they will be able to pay £5,000 for redecoration in three years' time. Starting now, they will invest a fixed sum of money at the beginning of each of the three years. The fund will earn 12% interest per annum. To the nearest £, what sum of money must be invested each year?

A £934
B £1,323
C £1,467
D £1,482

Circle your answer

A   B   C   D

21 A trade customer deducts a discount before paying £2,000 for goods which have an invoice value of £2,500. What percentage discount has been deducted?

A   15%
B   20%
C   25%
D   50%

Circle your answer

A   B   C   D

22 A company sells goods to a customer who is entitled to a trade discount of 5%. The invoice value of the goods, before discount, is £18,000. A settlement discount of 6% of net invoice value is offered if payment is made within 10 days of the invoice. If the customer settles after 5 days, how much will be received?

A   £16,020
B   £16,074
C   £16,920
D   £17,100

Circle your answer

A   B   C   D

23 Invoiced sales for a company in July amounted to £35,400 before discount. One half of all customers are expected to deduct a 2% settlement discount. One fifth of all sales are made to the trade at a discount of 10%. No-one will take both a trade discount and a settlement discount. There will be no bad debts. How much cash will be received in total from July sales?

A   £23,718
B   £24,426
C   £30,090
D   £34,338

Circle your answer

A   B   C   D

CHAPTER 5

THE COLLECTION AND PRESENTATION OF STATISTICAL DATA

This chapter covers the following topics:

- Sources of data
- Sampling
- Roundings, approximations and errors
- Presentation of data

1. Sources of data

1.1 The principal sources of data are:

(a) personal investigation
(b) teams of investigators
(c) questionnaires
(d) published statistics, including government publications
(e) historical records

1.2 If data are collected for a particular enquiry they are *primary data* of that enquiry. Data originally collected for some other purpose are *secondary data*. When using secondary data the definitions of variables and of the population must be carefully examined, because the aims of the person who originally collected the data may be quite different from those of later users of the data.

2. Sampling

2.1 If you wanted to find out something about a large population, such as the average salary in the UK, gathering data from every member of the population would be far too time-consuming and expensive. You would take a sample instead. The size of your sample depends on how sure you want to be that the results you obtain will be close to the true figures for the whole population. Many opinion polls rely on a sample of about a thousand people, for example.

2.2 There are several different ways of taking a sample

- *Random sampling* - every member of the population has an equal chance of being selected

- *Systematic sampling* - members of the population at regular intervals are selected. For example, one could take person number 23, person number 63, person number 103, and so on, taking every fortieth person. 40 is the *sampling interval*

- *Stratified sampling* - the population is broken up into layers (strata), and then a sample is taken from each layer. For example, in a survey of people's spending habits, you might first split the population into three layers, people earning £15,000 a year or less, people earning over £15,000 and up to £20,000 a year, and those earning over £20,000 a year, and then take a sample from each layer

- *Multi-stage sampling* - the population is broken down into groups, and groups are selected first before members of the population are sampled within those groups. This method differs from stratified sampling because the groups are not defined using a numerical scale, such as earnings, but could be for example geographical areas. For a survey of people in Britain, five counties could first be selected, and 200 people in each of those counties

- *Quota sampling* - interviewers are given a quota of a certain number of people to interview, perhaps broken down by age and sex. They then simply interview the first people they meet until they have fulfilled their quota, for example 50 males and 50 females

2.3 The choice of sampling method depends on

- how representative of the population the sample must be - the more important this is, the more random sampling is to be preferred

- whether particular sections of the population are of particular interest - stratified sampling can be used to concentrate on those sections

- the resources available - quota sampling is often cheapest

3. Roundings, approximations and errors

3.1 Many statistical results contain rounded figures. You should be able to quantify the possible error in rounded data. Thus if the average British salary is £13,000 to the nearest thousand pounds, the maximum error is £500 as the true figure could lie anywhere between £12,500 and £13,499.99.

3.2 It is sometimes useful to show the average error, since the maximum error will rarely occur. The average error for a *single item* is half of the maximum error.

> For a group of n items added together
>
> (a) for unbiased approximations (eg rounding to the nearest thousand pounds), the average error in total $= \sqrt{n} \times$ average error in individual items or values, as the errors on individual figures will partly, but not entirely, cancel each other out;
>
> (b) for biased approximations (eg rounding to the next thousand pounds above), the average error in total $= n \times$ average error in individual items or values, as the errors on individual figures are all in the same direction and cannot cancel each other out.

3.3 The seriousness of an error depends partly on the values of the data. If the average British salary is thought to be £13,500, and the average annual pocket money of British children is thought to be £50, an error of £30 would be much more serious in the latter case than in the former. *Relative error* makes this clear.

3.4 In the first case the relative error is $\dfrac{£30}{£13,500} \times 100\% = 0.22\%$

in the second case, it is $\dfrac{£30}{£50} \times 100\% = 60\%$.

4. Presentation of data

4.1 The first product of a survey is likely to be a list of numbers, for example annual turnovers of businesses. If the data are to be useful, they need to be presented in some more readable format.

4.2 *Tables*, laying out information in rows and columns, can be helpful. Here is an example.

Numbers (in thousands) of businesses of different sizes in Britain

| | | Annual turnover | | |
		Under £1m	£1m - £10m	Over £10m	Total
	North	500	200	75	775
Region	Midlands	700	250	80	1,030
	South	800	300	95	1,195
	Total	2,000	750	250	3,000

4.3 Data can also be presented in a summary as a frequency distribution. A *frequency distribution* lists the number of times different outcomes occur. For example, a restaurant might list the number of weeks in which one plate is broken, the number of weeks in which two plates are broken, and so on.

In a *grouped frequency distribution,* different outcomes are put in groups. For example, a restaurant could record the number of weeks in which 0-4 plates were broken, the number of weeks in which 5-9 plates were broken, and so on.

4.4 There are many different types of *chart* and *graph* which can be used to present data. A number of examples follow, in section 4.6. You might like to look at examples in newspapers and books, and ask yourself these questions.

● Is this the best type of chart for the job?

● Is the chart misleading in any way?

4.5 Before selecting a chart or graph for a job, we must think about the data we are presenting. In particular, we must be clear whether we are dealing with

(i) *continuous variables,* which can take on any value (for example, weight); or

(ii) *discrete variables,* which can only take on specified values (for example, number of children).

Attributes are characteristics which do not have numerical values, for example a person's sex.

4.6 (a) *Pie charts*
Pie charts are used to show the relative size of the components of a total. This is done by drawing a circle and splitting it into sectors so that the size of a sector is proportional to the component it represents.

(b) *Venn diagrams*
A Venn diagram may be used to show the divisions of a population, and how they overlap. For example, the following diagram shows how many out of a group of two hundred people like none, one or more than one of music, films and sport. 20 people like none of these, 15 like music and sport, but not films, 50 like films only, 25 + 10 + 5 + 15 = 55 like music (and possibly other things), and so on.

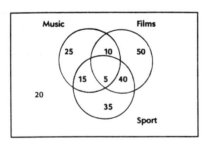

(c) *Bar charts*

Bar charts show the frequencies with which particular values of discrete variables, or particular attributes, occur, or the values attained by variables.

- In *simple bar charts*, there is one bar for each value or attribute, and the heights of the bars are proportional to the frequencies, or the values attained.

- In *multiple bar charts*, the heights of the bars are again proportional to the frequencies of the values attained, but bars are grouped together, for example by years. A multiple bar chart showing the sales of two products, P and Q, over two years might look like this:

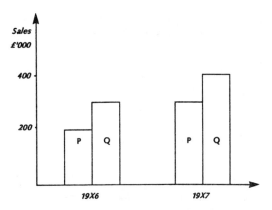

- In *compound bar charts*, each bar represents a total and is broken down into bands. The height of each band is proportional to the corresponding frequency or value attained. The first languages of people at an international conference held every year might be portrayed as follows:

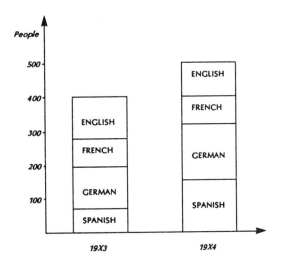

- *Percentage bar charts* are like compound bar charts except that all bars are the same height, and the heights of the bands show percentages of the total.

(d) *Histograms*

A histogram is used to show a frequency distribution of a continuous variable. The number of observations in each *class* (each range of values of the variable) is represented by the *area* covered by the bar, not by the height of the bar.

For example, we can draw a histogram to represent the following data.

Hours of production in a month		Number of
at least	less than	occasions
0	1,000	4
1,000	1,500	6
1,500	2,000	2

If we select 500 hours as a class interval, we then need to divide the frequency of the first group by two because it covers two class intervals:

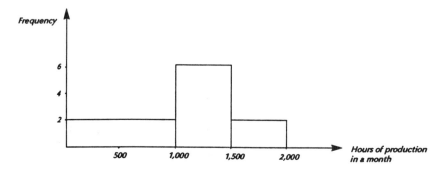

(e) *Ogives*

An *ogive or cumulative frequency curve* shows the number of observations less than or equal to a certain value because it shows the cumulative number of items with a value less than that value. An ogive for the above data concerning hours of production per week would be as follows:

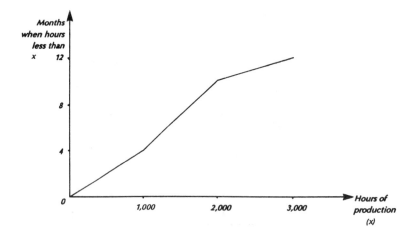

We can read off from an ogive the number of occasions on which the hours of production per week were less than any particular value.

Ogives can also be drawn to show the cumulative number of items with values more than a certain value. Such ogives slope down from left to right.

(f)   *Lorenz curves*

A Lorenz curve displays one cumulative amount against another. It shows the degree of concentration that a distribution might have. A common application is the examination of the distribution of wealth in the population.

We could, for example, arrange the whole population of Ruritania in order of wealth, starting with the poorest people. After going through the first 10% of people, we might find that between them they owned 2% of the total wealth. We might go on to find that the poorest 80% of people owned 25% of the total wealth, with the richest 20% of people owning 75% of the wealth.

An unequal distribution, such as this one, is reflected in a Lorenz curve by divergence from the diagonal. The greater the divergence, the more unequal is the distribution.

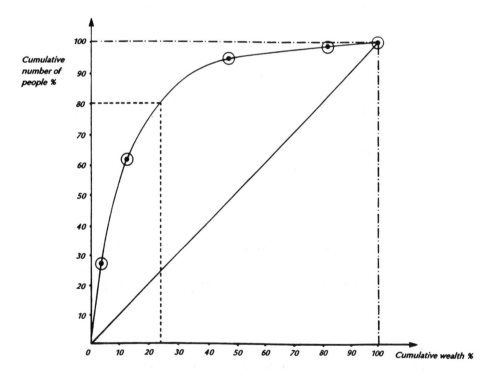

(g)   *Z charts*

A Z chart shows three sets of data and is so called because it looks like a letter Z. A typical Z chart is shown below.

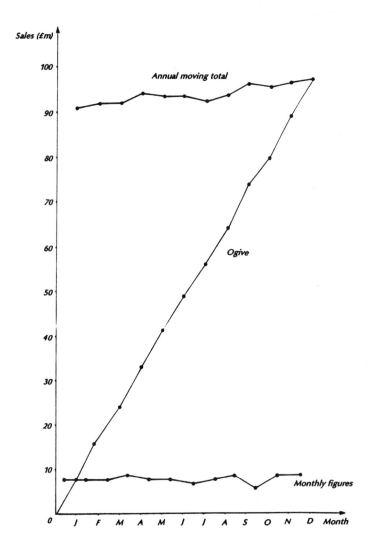

The three lines are:

(a) *monthly figures:* these show the monthly results together with any seasonal variations;

(b) *cumulative totals:* these show the performance in the part of the year to date, so that it can be compared with the performance required by the budget;

(c) *annual moving totals:* these show a comparison of the current levels of performance with those of the previous year. If the line is rising then this year's monthly results are better than the results of the corresponding month last year. The opposite applies if the line is falling.

One can of course prepare Z charts for daily, weekly or quarterly instead of monthly data.

QUESTIONS

1 Which of the following are secondary data sources?

Source
1. The Monthly Digest of Statistics published by the Central Statistical Office.
2. Economic Trends published by the Central Statistical Office.
3. Data collected for an attitude survey through personal interview, using a non-random sampling method.
4. Historical records of sales revenues to be used to prepare current forecasts.

A Sources 1 and 4 only
B Sources 1, 2 and 3 only
C Sources 1, 2 and 4 only
D Sources 3 and 4 only

Circle your answer

| A | B | C | D |

2 In which of the following publications would you find the Retail Prices Index?

A The Department of Employment Gazette
B The Blue Book on National Income and Expenditure
C Trade and Industry
D Economic Trends

Circle your answer

| A | B | C | D |

3 An interviewee selected for a survey has the following characteristics:

Characteristic
1. Sex = male
2. Height = 6 feet 2 inches
3. Marital status = single
4. Weight = 84kg

Which of these would be described as attributes?

A Characteristic 1 only
B Characteristic 3 only
C Characteristics 1 and 3 only
D Characteristics 2 and 4 only

Circle your answer

| A | B | C | D |

4   Identify the discrete variable or variables among the following.

Variable
1. Number of employees absent through illness per week
2. Number of customer complaints per month
3. Length of pipe laid per day by construction workers

A   Variables 1 and 3 only
B   Variables 1 and 2 only
C   Variable 3 only
D   Variables 2 and 3 only

Circle your answer

A	B	C	D

Data for questions 5 and 6

An accountant is selecting a sample of invoices for checking. The invoices are numbered sequentially. The first invoice is selected randomly and is invoice number 3. He then selects invoice numbers 7, 11, 15, 19 and 23 to complete the sample.

5   This type of sample is called

A   Multi-stage
B   Simple random
C   Stratified
D   Systematic

Circle your answer

A	B	C	D

6   What sampling interval was the accountant using?

A   3
B   4
C   6
D   20

Circle your answer

A	B	C	D

7 A marketing manager is selecting a sample of the company's customers for a survey. The customers have been sorted into five groups according to their annual sales value:

Annual sales		Number of customers
	up to £1,000	15
More than £1,000,	up to £10,000	20
More than £10,000,	up to £20,000	50
More than £20,000,	up to £30,000	25
More than £30,000		10

The manager then selects a 20% random sample from each of the five groups of customers. This type of sample is called

A   Cluster
B   Multi-stage
C   Simple random
D   Stratified

Circle your answer

| A | B | C | D |

8 A sample of employees have been interviewed for a pilot job appraisal scheme. To ensure that the sample contained the correct proportion of employees with varying lengths of service, a stratified random sample was used. Accordingly, the employees were divided into five strata:

Length of service		Number of employees
	up to 1 year	100
More than 1 year,	up to 3 years	365
More than 3 years,	up to 5 years	320
More than 5 years,	up to 10 years	120
More than 10 years		95

The personnel staff interviewed a sample of 200 people in total. How many of those interviewed would have been employed for up to 3 years?

A   40
B   73
C   93
D   157

Circle your answer

| A | B | C | D |

Data for questions 9 and 10

A company wishes to carry out a national survey of adults' reading habits. To reduce travelling costs, the country was first divided into constituencies. A sample of 50 constituencies was then selected at random. Within each of these constituencies, 5 polling districts were selected, again using random techniques. Interviewers will visit a random selection of 30 people on the electoral register in each of the districts selected.

9 What sampling method is the company using?

A Simple random
B Stratified
C Systematic
D Multi-stage

Circle your answer

A B C D

10 How many people will be interviewed?

A 150
B 250
C 1,500
D 7,500

Circle your answer

A B C D

11 In a particular sample survey, interviewers are provided with a set of specifications of the number of people of various kinds that they are required to interview:

	Male	Female	Total
Under 21 years	15	25	40
Over 21 years	26	43	69

The interviewers are free to select their own respondents, as long as they interview the correct number of each type.

What sampling method is being used?

A Multi-stage
B Quota
C Random
D Stratified

Circle your answer

A B C D

12 What is 726.586 to two decimal places?

A 726.58
B 726.59
C 726.60
D 727.00

Circle your answer

A B C D

13 What is 29.0354 to 3 significant figures?

A 29.0
B 29.03
C 29.04
D 29.035

Circle your answer

A   B   C   D

14 What is 504.20612 to 5 significant figures?

A 504.20
B 504.2061
C 504.20612
D 504.21

Circle your answer

A   B   C   D

Data for questions 15 - 17

A management report shows the production volumes of three factories for last month to be as follows:

Factory	Production volume (units)
North	9,000
South	14,000
West	8,000
Total	31,000

15 If each of the production volumes has been rounded to the nearest thousand units, within what limits does the true total production volume lie?

A 28,000 to 34,000 units
B 29,500 to 32,500 units
C 30,000 to 32,000 units
D 30,500 to 31,500 units

Circle your answer

A   B   C   D

16 If each of the production volumes has been rounded up to the nearest thousand units, within what limits does the true total production volume lie?

A 28,003 to 31,000 units
B 29,503 to 31,000 units
C 30,003 to 32,000 units
D 31,003 to 34,000 units

Circle your answer

A   B   C   D

17 If each of the production volumes has been rounded down to the nearest thousand units, within what limits does the true total production volume lie?

A 28,000 to 30,997 units
B 28,000 to 33,997 units
C 31,000 to 32,497 units
D 31,000 to 33,997 units

Circle your answer

A   B   C   D

Data for questions 18 and 19

Month	Sales value £'000
1	27
2	26
3	42
4	25
5	60
6	36
7	96
8	16
9	71
Total sales value	399

18 If each of the sales values has been rounded to the nearest thousand pounds, what is the average error in the figures for total sales value?

A ± £250
B ± £500
C ± £750
D ± £1,500

Circle your answer

A   B   C   D

19 If each of the sales values has been rounded up to the nearest thousand pounds, what is the average error in the figure for total sales value?

A £500
B £1,000
C £3,000
D £4,500

Circle your answer

A   B   C   D

Data for questions 20 - 22

The following sales data are available for the last 16 periods for a company. All figures are rounded to the nearest 10 units.

Period number	Sales units	Period number	Sales units	Period number	Sales units	Period number	Sales units
1	820	5	430	9	760	13	420
2	640	6	290	10	360	14	220
3	400	7	680	11	380	15	980
4	840	8	670	12	480	16	450

Total sales volume for 16 periods = 8,820 units.

20 What is the maximum absolute error in the total sales volume?

A ± 10 units
B ± 20 units
C ± 80 units
D ± 160 units

Circle your answer

A   B   C   D

21 What is the estimated average error in the total sales volume?

A ± 2.5 units
B ± 5 units
C ± 10 units
D ± 20 units

Circle your answer

A   B   C   D

22 What is the maximum relative error in the total sales volume?

A ± 0.1%
B ± 0.9%
C ± 1.0%
D ± 1.8%

Circle your answer

A   B   C   D

23 An accountant is forecasting the gross profit for next month. The sales manager has provided a sales estimate of £440,000. The production manager estimates that production costs will be £430,000. Both managers have rounded their forecasts to the nearest £10,000.

If the accountant uses the two estimates, what will be the maximum absolute error in the forecast profit figure?

A   £0
B ± £5,000
C ± £10,000
D ± £20,000

Circle your answer

A   B   C   D

24 A caterer intends to buy 450 doughnuts for 10p each and 275 cream buns for 20p each. The forecast quantities and prices are subject to errors of ± 8% and ± 10% respectively.

What is the maximum relative error on the caterer's forecast total expenditure?

A ± 10%
B ± 18%
C ± 18.8%
D ± 15.8%

Circle your answer

A   B   C   D

25 A company's planner is using the following forecasts to estimate the profit for next year:

	Forecast	Maximum relative error
	£'000	
Sales revenue	760	± 1%
Labour costs	240	± 5%
Material costs	280	± 6%
Other costs	180	± 3%

What will be the maximum relative error in the profit forecast?

A ± 6%
B ± 13%
C ± 15%
D ± 70%

Circle your answer

A   B   C   D

26 In a survey of the weights of solid materials dispensed by machines when black coffee with sugar was requested, the following results were obtained:

Numbers of machines dispensing given weights

		Sugar			
		< 5g	5g - < 10g	10g - < 15g	Total
	< 5g	37	46	28	111
Coffee	5g - <10g	45	72	60	177
	10g - <15g	12	50	14	76
	Total	94	168	102	364

How many machines definitely dispensed less than 20g in total?

A 168
B 200
C 240
D 350

Circle your answer

A   B   C   D

27 The following (as yet incomplete) table shows the sales achieved by a company's five shops over four weeks.

X Ltd sales in £ over first four weeks of 19X1

		Week				Total
		1	2	3	4	
	P	5,000	7,200		6,900	
	Q			8,000		
Shop	R	3,000	4,000	5,000		16,000
	S	2,700		6,000	5,000	20,000
	T	1,900	2,000		2,100	
	Total		25,400	28,000	25,500	96,500

What were the total sales of shop Q for the four weeks?

A £26,100
B £26,200
C £26,300
D £26,400

Circle your answer

A   B   C   D

28 The results of a survey of frequencies of telephone calls made in different geographical areas are to be tabulated. Which of the following would be a suitable choice of headings for the table?

A *Rows:* north, south; *Columns:* under 5 calls a day, 5 or more calls a day

B *Rows:* under 5 calls a day, over 5 calls a day; *Columns:* north, south

C *Rows:* under 5 calls a day, north; *Columns:* 5 or more calls a day, south

D *Rows:* under 5 calls a day, 5 or more but under 10 calls a day, over 10 calls a day; *Columns:* north, south

Circle your answer

A	B	C	D

29 The following frequency distribution shows the score achieved by students in a mathematics test:

Marks scored	Frequency
< 15	2
$\geqslant 15 \ < 40$	5
$\geqslant 40 \ < 60$	15
$\geqslant 60 \ < 80$	9
$\geqslant 80$	3

What percentage of students scored 60 marks or more?

A 12.0%
B 26.5%
C 35.3%
D 64.7%

Circle your answer

A	B	C	D

Data for questions 30 and 31

The following pie chart represents the total production costs for a factory for one month:

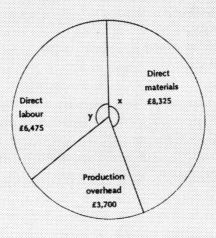

Direct materials £8,325

Direct labour £6,475

Production overhead £3,700

x

y

30 How large is the angle x in the pie chart?

A 160°
B 162°
C 164°
D 166°

Circle your answer

A   B   C   D

31 How large is the angle y in the pie chart?

A 122°
B 124°
C 126°
D 128°

Circle your answer

A   B   C   D

32 A market research survey of 280 people's opinions of three products, F, G and H, produced the following results:

15 people liked none of the products
120 people liked product F
160 people liked product G
100 people liked product H
50 people liked product F only
20 people liked products F and H only
28 people liked all three products

How many people liked product G only?

(A Venn diagram will help you to answer this question).

A   35
B   93
C   110
D   128

Circle your answer

A   B   C   D

33 A component bar chart showed the numbers of employees at each grade in a company on 31 December each year. The data were as follows:

Grade	Number of employees	
	19X5	19X6
1	20	25
2	57	65
3	180	220
4	1,200	1,450
5	663	670
	2,120	2,430

The bar for 19X5 was 10.6 cm high. How high was the segment for grade 4 employees for 19X6?

A   7.23 cm
B   7.24 cm
C   7.25 cm
D   7.26 cm

Circle your answer

A   B   C   D

34 One bar of a percentage bar chart showed the distribution of total sales revenue for a year between three divisions of a company. Division V's sales revenue was three times that of division W. Division W's sales revenue was twice that of division X. If the total height of the bar was 15 cm, how high was the segment corresponding to division W's sales?

A   2.50 cm
B   3.33 cm
C   3.75 cm
D   5.00 cm

Circle your answer

A   B   C   D

35 A company has recorded the following data on hours lost through employee lateness in a month.

Hours lost per employee		Number of employees
At least	less than	
0	12	9
12	16	15
16	20	9
20	28	6

Which of the following histograms represents these data?

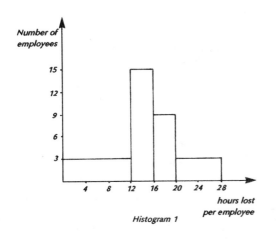

Histogram 1

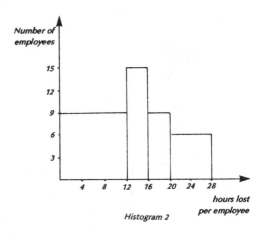

Histogram 2

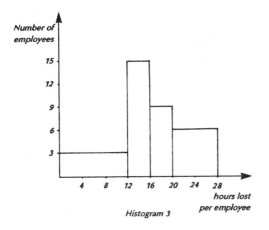

Histogram 3

Histogram 4

A   Histogram 1
B   Histogram 2
C   Histogram 3
D   Histogram 4

Circle your answer

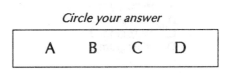

A   B   C   D

36 The following frequency distribution shows the weekly wages of the employees in a department:

Weekly wages(£)	Number of employees
> 80 ⩽ 120	4
>120 ⩽ 160	6
>160 ⩽ 180	6
>180 ⩽ 240	3

Which of the following histograms represents these data?

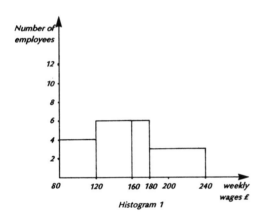

Histogram 1

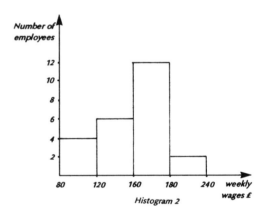

Histogram 2

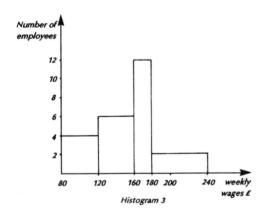

Histogram 3

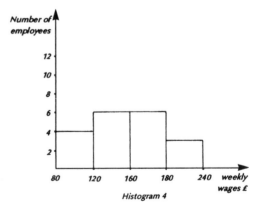

Histogram 4

A   Histogram 1
B   Histogram 2
C   Histogram 3
D   Histogram 4

Circle your answer

| A | B | C | D |

37 The following graph is an ogive of output per employee for one month.

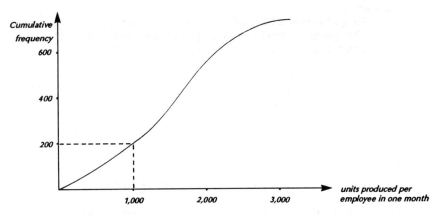

Which of the following statements about the month's production is/are correct?

Statement
1. 200 employees each produced less than 1,000 units
2. More than 400 employees achieved production of 1,000 units or more.
3. 200 employees each produced 1,000 units.

A Statement 1 only
B Statement 3 only
C Statements 1 and 2 only
D Statements 2 and 3 only

Circle your answer

A   B   C   D

38 The following ogive shows the number of times that weekly output exceeded a certain value over a period of 80 weeks:

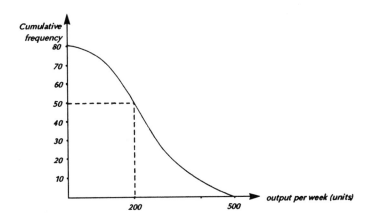

Which of the following statements is/are correct?

Statement
1. Output exceeded 200 units in each of 50 weeks.
2. There were 50 weeks in which production totalled 200 units.
3. Output was 200 units or less in each of 50 weeks.

A   Statement 1 only
B   Statement 2 only
C   Statement 3 only
D   Statements 2 and 3 only

Circle your answer

| A | B | C | D |

39 A manager wishes to receive the following information about sales values on a regular basis:

(a)   the monthly totals, so that he can see seasonal variations;
(b)   the totals for sales achieved in the year to date;
(c)   a comparison of the current levels of performance with those of the previous year.

Which of the following graphs or charts would best present this information pictorially?

A   An ogive combined with a histogram
B   A Z chart
C   A Lorenz curve
D   Two ogives

Circle your answer

| A | B | C | D |

40 A company has drawn the following Lorenz curve to represent the distribution of sales by customer over the last two years:

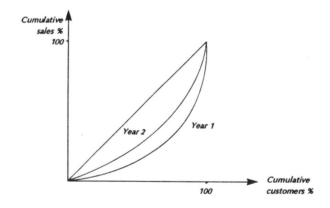

Which of the following statements is/are correct?

Statement
1. The company has many equally important customers which together account for nearly all sales.
2. The company has a small number of customers which account for a substantial proportion of total sales.
3. In year 2 the sales were spread more evenly over the total number of customers than in year 1.

A   Statement 1 only
B   Statements 1 and 3 only
C   Statements 2 and 3 only
D   Statement 3 only

Circle your answer

A	B	C	D

CHAPTER 6

PROBABILITY

This chapter covers the following topics:

- Basic ideas of probability
- Combinations and permutations
- The binomial, normal and Poisson distributions
- Confidence intervals
- Decision trees

1. Basic ideas of probability

1.1 The methods of probability are about putting some of our everyday statements into mathematical form, so we can draw conclusions from them. For example, you might say that it will probably rain today, because it is October and it often rains in October. That is enough for you to conclude that you should take an umbrella, but if you are a farmer trying to work out the likely effect on your potato yield, you need something in numerical terms. You need to know the *probabilities* of different outcomes. These are precise figures for the chance of something (called an *outcome)* happening. For example, there might be a 60% (= 0.6) chance that the rainfall on 1 October will be more than 2mm. We can put this into a convenient shorthand as follows.

(i)   Give the outcome a name: say C = rain on 1 October is more than 2mm.
(ii)   State the fact that the probability of outcome C is 0.6 as P(C) = 0.6.

1.2 Because probabilities correspond to the chances of something happening, there are limits to the values probabilities can have.

(i)   No probability can be less than zero. A probability of zero means there is no chance of the corresponding outcome happening.

(ii)   No probability can be greater than 1 (or 100%). A probability of 1 (or 100%) means that the corresponding outcome will certainly happen.

1.3 Where there are a number of possible outcomes, we would often like to have a complete list of the outcomes and the probabilities of their occurring. Such a list is called a *probability distribution.*

Going back to possible rainfalls on 1 October, we could have a probability distribution as follows:

Outcome		Probability
Rainfall (mm)	Name	
1 or less	A	0.1
More than 1, up to 2	B	0.3
Over 2	C	0.6
		$\overline{1.0}$

Note that the probabilities add up to 1. This is because precisely one of the outcomes will occur. There must be some level of rainfall, even if it is zero (covered by outcome A), and whatever level it is will correspond to just one outcome (precisely 2mm, for example, is covered by outcome B and not by outcome C).

1.4 We may be interested in the probability of several things all happening. For example, you may have placed a bet under which you will win £5,000 if a horse called Eclipse wins the Derby *and* when you go back to the bookmaker and he tosses a coin, it comes down heads. We call the things which have outcomes *events* or *trials*. 'Trials' is the more usual term when there are several very similar trials. We will use 'events' here because the two events are very different: they are a horse race and a toss of a coin.

The events here have the following possible outcomes:

Derby: A = Eclipse wins
                B = Eclipse does not win

Toss of coin: H = coin comes down heads
                T = coin comes down tails

The events are *independent,* ie the outcome of one cannot influence the outcome of the other. We can therefore apply the following rule:

> The probability that two outcomes, X and Y, of two independent events will both occur is the product of the probabilities of each of the events:
> $$P(X \text{ and } Y) = P(X) \times P(Y)$$

In our example, if P(A) = 0.3 and P(H) = 0.5, the probability of your winning £5,000 is
$$P(A \text{ and } H) = P(A) \times P(H) = 0.3 \times 0.5 = 0.15.$$

1.5 It may be that two events are not independent. For example, if one event is a horse race on Monday, and the other is another race involving the same horses on Tuesday, and you are thinking of placing a bet on a horse called Nijinsky to win the race on Tuesday, you would think it much more likely that he would win if he had won Monday's race than if he had not. We then need the following rule:

> P(X and Y) = P(X) x P(Y|X)
>   or P(Y) x P(X|Y)
>
> where P(Y|X) is the probability that Y will happen, given that X happens
>   P(X|Y) is the probability that X will happen, given that Y happens

1.6 Sometimes we want the probability of any one or more of a set of outcomes occurring, without caring precisely which outcomes occur. How we get our answer depends on whether or not the outcomes we are interested in are mutually exclusive.

1.7 Outcomes are *mutually exclusive* if no more than one of them can occur. For example, a horse cannot in one race come first and second, or second and third, or first and third, so the outcomes of that horse coming first, coming second and coming third are mutually exclusive. You might want to know the probability of any one of these outcomes occurring, without caring which one occurs, because you are thinking of betting on the horse coming in the first three. To get this probability, simply add the probabilities of the individual outcomes.

> The probabilities of any one of two or more mutually exclusive outcomes occurring is the sum of the probabilities of the individual outcomes.

1.8 If outcomes are not mutually exclusive, we have to modify this rule as follows.

> If X and Y are two outcomes, the probability of either or both of them occurring is given by:
>
> $$P(X \text{ or } Y) = P(X) + P(Y) - P(X \text{ and } Y)$$

We subtract P(X and Y) so as to avoid counting this possibility twice. We could set out the possibilities like this:

	Y	Not Y
X	X and Y	X but not Y
Not X	Y but not X	Neither X nor Y

P(X) covers the top row, and P(Y) covers the left hand column. Between them, they cover the top left hand corner (X and Y) twice, so we have to deduct P(X and Y) once to avoid counting it twice.

1.9 An *expected value* is an average, derived from probabilities, of possible outcomes which are themselves expressed in numerical terms. Here is an example.

Sales revenue £	Probability	Revenue × probability £
1,000	0.1	100
3,000	0.7	2,100
5,000	0.2	1,000
	1.0	
Expected value of sales revenue		3,200

2. Combinations and permutations

2.1 Probability questions often hinge on the number of different ways something can happen, and on the proportion of those different ways which meet some criterion. For this reason, combinations and permutations are often relevant.

2.2 A combination is a set of items, selected from a larger collection of items, regardless of the order in which they are selected. We refer to the number of possible combinations of r items from n items. For example, suppose that four people, E, F, G and H, apply for two vacancies as managers. The different possible combinations to fill the two posts from the four applicants would be EF, EG, EH, FG, FH and GH. There are six possible combinations.

2.3 There is a formula that we can use to calculate the number of combinations.

$$_nC_r = \frac{n!}{(n-r)!r!}$$

The notation $_nC_r$ means 'the number of different combinations of r items from a set of n items'

Using this formula in the problem in paragraph 2.2, we would have:

$$_4C_2 = \frac{4!}{(4-2)!2!} = \frac{4 \times 3 \times 2 \times 1}{2 \times 1 \times 2 \times 1} = 6 \text{ combinations.}$$

2.4 Because there are six combinations, the probability of any one combination (say EF) being selected would, if the selection were random, be 1/6.

2.5 A permutation is a set of items, selected from a collection of items, in which the order of selection or arrangement is significant. We refer to the number of possible permutations of r items from n items.

2.6 For example, in the problem in paragraph 2.2, suppose that the two vacancies were for the posts of senior manager and junior manager. The order of selection would be important and the possible permutations would be:

Senior	Junior
E	F
E	G
E	H
F	E
F	G
F	H
G	E
G	F
G	H
H	E
H	F
H	G

There are 12 possible permutations.

2.7 Once again, there is a formula.

$$_nP_r = \frac{n!}{(n-r)!}$$

The notation $_nP_r$ means 'the number of different permutations of r items from a set of n items'

Using this formula in the problem in paragraph 2.5, we would have:

$$_4P_2 = \frac{4!}{(4-2)!} = \frac{4 \times 3 \times 2 \times 1}{2 \times 1} = 12 \text{ permutations.}$$

3. Probability distributions

3.1 A knowledge of *specific* probability distributions is not needed for some examinations. The following outline notes are meant as memory-joggers for students who do need such knowledge and who have already learnt the topic from study manuals.

3.2 The binomial probability distribution applies when any trial (the word often used for events when there is a series of similar events) can have one of two outcomes (often called success and failure), and the probability of a success on any one trial (p) is constant. The probability of a failure on any one trial, 1 - p, is denoted by q.

The probability of r successes in n trials is

$$_nC_r \, p^r \, q^{n-r} = \frac{n!}{(n-r)!r!} p^r \, q^{n-r}$$

The mean of the binomial distribution is np.

The standard deviation of the binomial distribution is $\sqrt{npq}$

3.3 The normal distribution can be regarded as a probability distribution in its own right. For example, if the weights of elephants are normally distributed with a mean of 5,000 kg and a standard deviation of 300 kg the probability of a randomly chosen elephant weighing more than 5,450 kg, ie more than 1.5 standard deviations above the mean, is (from normal distribution tables given at the end of this book) 0.5 - 0.4332 = 0.0668 = 6.68%.

3.4 The normal distribution can also be used as an approximation to the binomial distribution, when n is large (*say,* over 30) and p is reasonably near 0.5. The mean and standard deviation to use are np and $\sqrt{npq}$. Parts of the binomial distribution (eg 'over 50 successes') can then be translated into areas more or less than a certain number of standard deviations away from the mean, and normal distribution tables can then be used.

3.5 The Poisson distribution is a probability distribution in its own right, and can also be used as an approximation to the binomial distribution when n is large (*say,* over 30) and p is small. Values for the Poisson distribution are given in tables at the end of this book.

If, for example, the mean number of cars passing a house in any one hour is 1.7, and the Poisson distribution applies, the tables tell us that the probability of two cars passing the house in an hour is 0.264.

When the Poisson distribution is used as an approximation to the binomial distribution, the mean to use is np.

4. Confidence intervals

4.1 A knowledge of confidence intervals is only required for a few foundation level examinations (eg. CIMA). These notes are meant as memory-joggers for those who have already learnt the topic.

4.2 If we take a random sample (of at least 30) from a population, and measure some variable (say income), it is likely that the sample mean will be reasonably close to the population mean. The standard error measures how spread out the means of all possible samples are around the population mean, so it helps to give an idea of how far out we might be if we assume that the population mean equals the sample mean.

> If s = sample standard deviation
> n = size of sample
>
> Then standard error of the mean = $\dfrac{s}{\sqrt{n}}$

4.3 We could take a sample and see what proportion of its members had some attribute, say left-handedness. As with means, we can measure how spread out the proportions in all possible samples are around the population proportion.

> If p = sample proportion
> n = size of sample
>
> Then standard error of the proportion = $\sqrt{\dfrac{p(1-p)}{n}}$

4.4 We can go on to state a range within which the population mean or proportion lies, and to say how confident we are of being right.

> 95% confidence interval:
>
> We can be 95% confident that the population mean (or proportion) lies in the interval
>
> Sample mean (or proportion) ± 1.96 standard errors.

For 99% confidence, use the same formula but with 2.58 instead of 1.96

5. Decision trees

5.1 Decision trees are diagrams showing how a project can unfold. At each point of branching, either a decision is made, for example on how much to spend on advertising, or a set of possible outcomes outside our control but with known probabilities, for example levels of demand, is considered. Once the tree is completed, expected value calculations are used to find the best decision at each stage, working from right to left through the tree.

5.2 A decision tree might look like this.

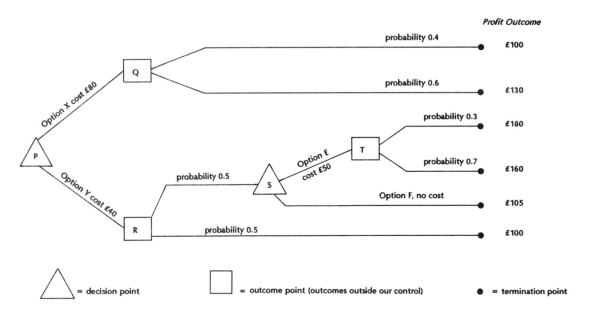

QUESTIONS

1 An analysis of 480 working days in a factory shows that on 360 days there were no machine breakdowns. Assuming that this pattern will continue, what is the probability that there will be a machine breakdown on any particular day?

A 12%
B 25%
C 33%
D 75%

Circle your answer

A   B   C   D

2 A distributor has recorded the following demand for a stock item over the last 200 days:

Daily demand units	Number of days
50	27
51	35
52	39
53	42
54	57

If these data are representative of the normal pattern of sales, what is the probability of a daily demand of 53 units?

A 20%
B 21%
C 42%
D 84%

Circle your answer

A   B   C   D

3 A production director is responsible for overseeing the operations of three factories - North, South and West. He visits one factory per week. He visits the West factory as often as he visits the North factory, but he visits the South factory twice as often as he visits the West factory.

What is the probability that in any one week he will visit the North factory?

A 0.17
B 0.20
C 0.25
D 0.33

Circle your answer

A   B   C   D

93

Data for questions 4 - 6

Product Y passes through a production line of four consecutive processes before it is completed. In each process, some units are rejected and scrapped. Data for a typical month are as follows:

		units
Input to production line		4,000
Rejects:		
	process 1	420
	process 2	208
	process 3	125
	process 4	87

4   What is the probability that a unit, once started, will become a completed unit of finished product Y?

A   21.0%
B   26.6%
C   79.0%
D   84.0%

Circle your answer

A   B   C   D

5   What is the probability that a unit will enter process 3?

A   3.1%
B   15.7%
C   81.2%
D   84.3%

Circle your answer

A   B   C   D

6   What is the probability that a unit entering process 3 will be scrapped in that process?

A   0.031
B   0.037
C   0.040
D   0.188

Circle your answer

A   B   C   D

7 A company is deciding whether to invest in a project. There are three possible outcomes of the investment:

Outcome	Resulting Profit/(Loss) £'000
Optimistic	19.2
Most likely	12.5
Pessimistic	(6.7)

There is a 30% chance of the optimistic outcome, and a 60% chance of the most likely outcome arising.

The expected value of profit from the project is:

A £8,333
B £9,150
C £12,590
D £13,260

Circle your answer

| A | B | C | D |

8 A company manufactures a product which has a selling price of £14 per unit. Fixed costs incurred are £9,400 per period. Sales demand and unit variable costs are uncertain, but the following forecasts have been prepared for the next period:

Demand (units)	Probability	Variable cost per unit (£)	Probability
4,000	0.2	8.50	0.4
6,500	0.7	9.00	0.6
3,000	0.1		

The unit variable costs are unaffected by the sales demand.

What is the expected value of profit from this product for the next period?

A £19,980
B £20,263
C £29,380
D £40,320

Circle your answer

| A | B | C | D |

9 A company wishes to appoint three representatives for a new overseas sales force. Applications have been received from nine suitably qualified and experienced people. In how many different ways could the new sales force be selected?

A 27
B 81
C 84
D 504

Circle your answer

| A | B | C | D |

95

An award committee is selecting two examination candidates to receive prize awards. Eight candidates have performed sufficiently well to be considered for a prize.

10 In how many different ways could the two prizewinners be selected from the eight candidates?

A 16
B 28
C 32
D 56

Circle your answer

A   B   C   D

11 If the two awards are to be designated first prize and second prize, in how many different ways could they be awarded among the eight candidates?

A 14
B 16
C 28
D 56

Circle your answer

A   B   C   D

The board of directors of Choosit Limited wish to select four out of seven proposed projects in which to invest next year.

12 In how many ways can four out of seven projects be selected?

A 35
B 140
C 210
D 840

Circle your answer

A   B   C   D

13 If the board is already committed to one project out of the seven, in how many ways could the four projects now be selected?

A 20
B 34
C 40
D 120

Circle your answer

A   B   C   D

14 Four of the projects are high risk projects, and the other three are medium risk projects. The board must select at least two medium risk projects, but is not committed to any one project. In how many ways could the four projects now be selected?

A 14
B 18
C 22
D 72

Circle your answer

A   B   C   D

Data for questions 15 and 16

A systems analyst is devising a computerised accounts coding system. She is using the digits 0 - 9 inclusive to form 3-digit account numbers. No digit can be used more than once in a number so that, for instance, 122 and 474 are not acceptable account numbers.

15 How many account numbers can there be, at most, in the complete system?

A 120
B 504
C 720
D 900

Circle your answer

A   B   C   D

16 The analyst intends to use account numbers beginning with 4 for capital expenditure items. How many such account numbers will be available?

A 56
B 72
C 99
D 100

Circle your answer

A   B   C   D

17 The delivery of an item of raw material from a supplier may take up to five weeks from the time the order is placed. The probabilities of delivery periods are as follows:

Delivery period	Probability
Up to one week	0.20
>1 week ⩽ 2 weeks	0.30
>2 weeks ⩽ 3 weeks	0.10
>3 weeks ⩽ 4 weeks	0.25
>4 weeks ⩽ 5 weeks	0.15

What is the probability of a delivery period of more than three weeks?

A   0.25
B   0.40
C   0.50
D   0.60

Circle your answer

A   B   C   D

Data for questions 18 and 19

A butcher knows that the sales demand for fresh chickens is 14, 15 or 16 chickens per day. The probability of demand is:

Demand per day	Probability
14 chickens	0.5
15 chickens	0.3
16 chickens	0.2

Demand on any day is independent of demand on any other day.

18 What is the probability that demand will be 15 chickens per day for two consecutive days?

A   0.09
B   0.30
C   0.60
D   0.90

Circle your answer

A   B   C   D

19 What is the probability that demand will be 14 chickens on each of days 1 and day 2, and 16 chickens on day 3?

A 0.045
B 0.05
C 0.1
D 0.12

Circle your answer

A   B   C   D

20 A company sells two products, G and H, and each product's sales are independent of the other product's. Monthly sales volumes vary according to the following probabilities:

Product G		Product H	
Sales units	Probability	Sales units	Probability
100	0.35	100	0.25
200	0.15	250	0.45
300	0.50	300	0.30

What is the probability that either product G or product H will achieve sales of 300 units in any month?

A 0.15
B 0.20
C 0.65
D 0.80

Circle your answer

A   B   C   D

21 The accountant of Spendthrift Limited is concerned about cash flow. He has warned the directors that there is a 60% probability that the bank overdraft limit will be exceeded if extended supplier credit cannot be negotiated. The limit will not be exceeded if such credit can be negotiated. The purchasing manager has estimated that the probability of success in negotiating extended credit is only 25%. The probability that the overdraft limit will be exceeded is:

A 0.15
B 0.35
C 0.45
D 0.85

Circle your answer

A   B   C   D

Data for questions 22 - 24

A factory has three machines, L, M and N, each of which produces completed glass containers from raw materials. An inspector is three times as likely to sample from machine M as he is from Machine L, and twice as likely to sample from machine N as he is from machine M. The proportions of defective output from the three machines are:

L 10%   M 20%   N 25%

22 What is the probability that a container selected by the inspector is from machine L?

A 0.01
B 0.10
C 0.17
D 0.20

Circle your answer

| A | B | C | D |

23 What is the probability that a container selected by the inspector is defective?

A 0.05
B 0.21
C 0.22
D 0.55

Circle your answer

| A | B | C | D |

24 What is the probability that a defective container selected by the inspector comes from machine N?

A 0.15
B 0.45
C 0.60
D 0.68

Circle your answer

| A | B | C | D |

Data for questions 25 and 26

Cricket matches are arranged every Saturday in summer in a certain village, but sometimes they are cancelled, because of rain, illness or other reasons. The probability of rain on any Saturday in summer is 0.45. The probability of a match being cancelled if it rains is 0.9, and the probability of a match being cancelled if it does not rain is 0.2. Draw up a table of all possibilities (rain or no rain, match played or match cancelled) and fill in figures for 1,000 arranged matches, then use it to answer questions 25 and 26.

25 If a match is cancelled, what is the probability that it rained on the Saturday in question?

A 0.79
B 0.87
C 0.88
D 0.91

Circle your answer

| A | B | C | D |

26 If a match was played, what is the probability that it did not rain on the Saturday in question?

A 0.79
B 0.87
C 0.88
D 0.91

Circle your answer

A   B   C   D

Data for questions 27 - 29

Answer questions 27 -29 by drawing Venn diagrams, with two overlapping circles, one for each outcome. Fill in probabilities from the information given, then find the required probability, using the fact that all the probabilities on the diagram must add up to 1.

---

27 Two outcomes are denoted E and F. $\bar{E}$ denotes 'not E' and $\bar{F}$ denotes 'not F'. P denotes probability.

$P(\bar{E}$ or $\bar{F}) = 0.7$ $P(\bar{E}$ and $\bar{F}) = 0.2$ $P(F) = 0.4$

What is the P(E)?

A 0.4
B 0.5
C 0.7
D 0.9

Circle your answer

A   B   C   D

---

28 Two outcomes are denoted X and Y. $\bar{Y}$ denotes 'not Y'. P denotes probability.

$P(X) = 0.40$ $P(Y) = 0.30$ $P(X$ and $Y) = 0.05$

$P(X|\bar{Y})$ is

A 0.35
B 0.45
C 0.50
D 0.53

Circle your answer

A   B   C   D

29 Two outcomes are denoted M and N. $\bar{M}$ denotes 'not M' and $\bar{N}$ denotes 'not N'. P denotes probability:

$P(M) = 0.50$ $P(M \text{ and } N) = 0.15$ $P(\bar{M} \text{ and } \bar{N}) = 0.10$

$P(N)$ is

A   0.075
B   0.25
C   0.35
D   0.55

Circle your answer

| A | B | C | D |

Data for questions 30 - 31

A market researcher has established that one in three cyclists uses Everglow batteries in their cycle lamps. He then selects two cyclists at random to interview about their batteries.

30 What is the probability that at least one of the cyclists interviewed uses Everglow batteries?

A   1/9
B   2/9
C   4/9
D   5/9

Circle your answer

| A | B | C | D |

31 What is the probability that exactly one of the cyclists interviewed uses Everglow batteries?

A   1/9
B   2/9
C   4/9
D   5/9

Circle your answer

| A | B | C | D |

Data for questions 32 - 35

A company owns two electric delivery vehicles, vehicle V and vehicle W. The vehicles are used during the day and their batteries are recharged at night. Each vehicle should be capable of travelling thirty miles in a day, but experience has shown that the probabilities of the vehicles achieving this mileage are:

Vehicle	Probability of being able to go 30 miles in a day
V	7/8
W	2/3

32 What is the probability that the vehicles will each be able to go 30 miles in any one day?

A 1/24
B 9/24
C 11/24
D 14/24

Circle your answer

A   B   C   D

33 The probability that at least one vehicle will be able to go 30 miles in any one day is

A 7/24
B 13/24
C 14/24
D 23/24

Circle your answer

A   B   C   D

34 The probability that only vehicle V will be able to go 30 miles in any one day is

A 7/24
B 13/24
C 7/8
D 22/24

Circle your answer

A   B   C   D

35 What is the probability that exactly one vehicle will be able to go 30 miles in any one day?

A   5/24
B   9/24
C   14/24
D   23/24

Circle your answer

A   B   C   D

Data for questions 36 and 37

The independent probabilities that an error will be made on any one day by three different workers are 15%, 20% and 30% respectively.

36 The probability that there will be at least one error made on any particular day is

A   47.6%
B   52.4%
C   64.1%
D   65.0%

Circle your answer

A   B   C   D

37 The probability that exactly one error will be made on any particular day is

A   40.7%
B   52.4%
C   64.1%
D   65.0%

Circle your answer

A   B   C   D

38 A manufacturer assembles a toy from ten independently produced components, each of which has a probability of 0.01 of being defective. If any one component is defective, the whole toy is defective. The probability of a toy being defective is

A $(0.01)^{10}$
B   0.10
C $(0.99)^{10}$
D $1 - (0.99)^{10}$

Circle your answer

A   B   C   D

39 In one day, a department manufactures four products, each of which has an independent chance of 20% being faulty. The probability that at least three products are *not* faulty is

A 0.1024
B 0.5120
C 0.8192
D 0.9216

Circle your answer

A   B   C   D

40 A specialist shop attracts five customers per day. There is an independent probability of 1/3 that any one customer will make a purchase. The probability that the shop will make *at most* one sale in a day is

A 16/243
B 48/243
C 85/243
D 112/243

Circle your answer

A   B   C   D

41 The probability of a high jumper clearing 1.8m on any one jump is 0.6. What is the probability of his clearing 1.8m in precisely three out of seven jumps?

A 0.006
B 0.194
C 0.273
D 0.290

Circle your answer

A   B   C   D

42 The lives of ball point pens are normally distributed, with a mean of 20,000 words and a standard deviation of 6,000 words. What proportion of ball point pens have a life of over 26,000 words? (Use the normal distribution tables at the end of this book.)

A 0.1587
B 0.25
C 0.3413
D 0.3984

Circle your answer

A   B   C   D

43 If the value of a random variable is normally distributed, what is the probability of its taking a value between 0.7 standard deviations below the mean and 1.8 standard deviations above the mean?

A 0.2779
B 0.5359
C 0.7221
D 0.742

Circle your answer

A   B   C   D

44 The salaries of a group of 1,000 employees are normally distributed, with a mean of £14,500. If 305 of the employees have salaries below £12,500, what is the standard deviation of the distribution?

A £1,020
B £1,220
C £3,279
D £3,922

Circle your answer

A   B   C   D

45 In a binomial distribution, n = 300 and p = 0.4. What is the approximate probability of at least 125 successes? Use tables to derive your answer.

A 0.1331
B 0.2224
C 0.2776
D 0.3669

Circle your answer

A   B   C   D

46 A gambler plays a game of chance 150 times. On each play, he has a probability of 0.45 of winning. What is the approximate probability of his winning between 62 and 70 times?

A 0.41
B 0.475
C 0.525
D 0.59

Circle your answer

A   B   C   D

47 The number of 'wrong number' calls received on any one day on a certain telephone follows a Poisson distribution, with a mean of 2.2. What is the probability of three or more such calls being received on any one day?

A 0.1807
B 0.1966
C 0.3773
D 0.4881

Circle your answer

A   B   C   D

48 A rope factory inspects all output for defects. The number of defects per km of rope follows a Poisson distribution, with a mean of 0.8 defects per km. What is the probability of 4 defects in any 3 km of rope?

A 0.0077
B 0.0231
C 0.0308
D 0.1254

Circle your answer

A   B   C   D

49 In a binomial distribution, n = 500 and p = 0.0032. What is the approximate probability of either one or two successes?

A   0.2167
B   0.4186
C   0.5814
D   0.7833

Circle your answer

A   B   C   D

50 The mean weight per person of a sample of 50 women was 53kg, and the sample standard deviation was 12 kg. What is the 95% confidence interval for the mean weight of all women?

A   50.2 kg to 55.8 kg
B   49.67 kg to 56.33 kg
C   49.05 kg to 56.95 kg
D   48.62 kg to 57.38 kg

Circle your answer

A   B   C   D

51 The weights of bags of sugar produced by a factory have a standard deviation of 15g. A sample is to be taken, to determine the mean weight to within 2g with 95% confidence. How many bags should there be in the sample?

A   111
B   217
C   221
D   285

Circle your answer

A   B   C   D

52 In a sample of 80 voters, 36 said they thought there would be a change of government at the next general election. What is the 99% confidence interval for the proportion of all voters who think there will be such a change?

A   0.45 ± 0.092
B   0.45 ± 0.109
C   0.45 ± 0.130
D   0.45 ± 0.144

Circle your answer

A   B   C   D

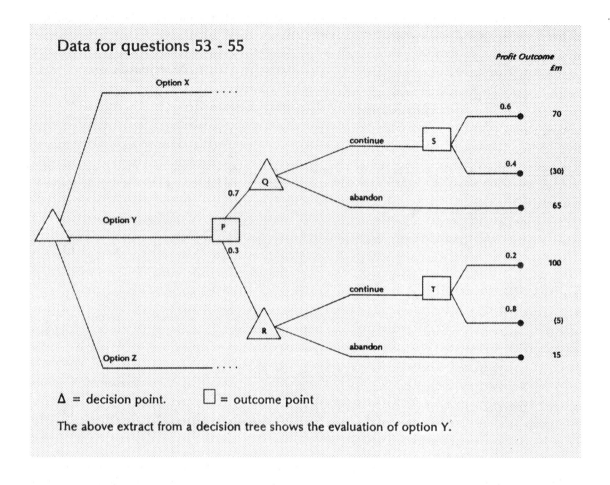

Data for questions 53 - 55

Profit Outcome
£m

Option X . . . .

continue ——— S
0.6 ● 70
0.4 ● (30)

Q 0.7

abandon ——— 65

P

Option Y

0.3

continue ——— T
0.2 ● 100
0.8 ● (5)

R

abandon ——— 15

Option Z . . . .

Δ = decision point. ☐ = outcome point

The above extract from a decision tree shows the evaluation of option Y.

53 What is the expected value of the decision at point Q, assuming the decision giving the highest expected value is made?

A £30m
B £65m
C £89m
D £105m

Circle your answer

| A | B | C | D |

54 What is the expected value of the decision at point R, assuming the decision giving the highest expected value is made?

A £15m
B £16m
C £95m
D £110m

Circle your answer

| A | B | C | D |

55
What is the expected value of option Y, assuming the decision giving the highest expected value is made at any subsequent decision point?

A £25.8m
B £30.0m
C £50.3m
D £106.5m

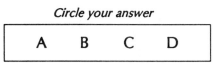

Circle your answer

A   B   C   D

Data for questions 56 and 57

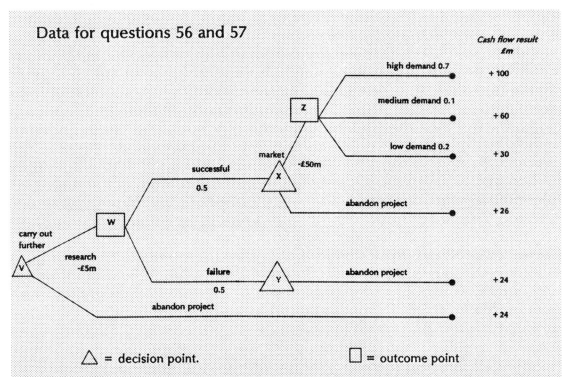

△ = decision point.   ☐ = outcome point

In the above decision tree, decision point V represents the decision whether to carry out further research on a project, at a cost of £5m, or to abandon the project. Decision point X represents the decision whether to market the successful product of the research, at a cost of £50m, or to abandon the project. Three possible demands could result if the company decides to market the product, shown at outcome point Z.

56
What is the expected value at decision point X, assuming the decision giving the highest expected value is made?

A £26m
B £32m
C £82m
D £107m

Circle your answer

A   B   C   D

109

57 At decision point V, what is the expected value of the decision to carry out further research, assuming the decision giving the highest expected value is made at any subsequent decision point?

A   £4m
B   £23m
C   £28m
D   £53m

Circle your answer

| A | B | C | D |

CHAPTER 7

AVERAGES AND DISPERSION.
CORRELATION AND REGRESSION

This chapter covers the following topics:

- Averages
- Dispersion
- Correlation and regression

1. Averages

1.1 An average is a *measure of central tendency*. The values of a variable may spread over a range, but these values cluster around a central point. This central point, or average, is in some way representative of the population as a whole. The most important averages are the arithmetic mean, the mode and the median.

1.2 The arithmetic mean is the best known type of average.

$$\text{Arithmetic mean} = \bar{x} = \frac{\text{Sum of the values of items}}{\text{Number of items}}$$

The symbol $\bar{x}$ is used to denote the arithmetic mean.

If data are given in a frequency distribution, this formula is amended slightly:

$$\text{Arithmetic mean} = \bar{x} = \frac{\Sigma fx}{n} = \frac{\Sigma fx}{\Sigma f}$$

f = frequency of a class (= number of items in that class)
x = value of each item in that class
n = Σf = total number of items.

1.3 Where data are given in a grouped frequency distribution and the groups each cover a range of values, the mid-point of each range is used as the value of each item in the class.

1.4 The *mode* is the most frequently occurring value. For example, the numbers of people in a town taking different shoe sizes might be as follows:

Shoe size	Number of people
6	4,000
7	8,000
8	2,000
	14,000

The mode will be size 7 because it is the value which occurs most frequently. A shoe shop could use this information in deciding which size to stock most of.

1.5 In a grouped frequency distribution, the mode can only be estimated approximately. The method of making this estimate is as follows.

(i) Establish which is the class interval with the highest frequency. This is called the *modal class*.

(ii) Apply the following formula:

$$\text{Mode} = L + \frac{(F_1 - F_0) \times c}{2F_1 - F_0 - F_2}$$

$$\text{Where} \quad L = \text{lower limit of modal class}$$
$$F_0 = \text{frequency of the next class below the modal class}$$
$$F_1 = \text{frequency of the modal class}$$
$$F_2 = \text{frequency of the next class above the modal class}$$
$$c = \text{width of the modal class}$$

Note that this formula requires that the modal class and the two classes either side of it be of equal width. A graphical method, which can be used where this is not so, is illustrated in question 18.

1.6 The *median* is the value of the middle member of a list of items arranged in order of size. Where there is an even number of members, then the median is the average of the two members on either side of the middle. The middle item of a distribution is the $\frac{(n+1)\text{th}}{2}$ item where n is the number of items.

1.7 The median of a set of ungrouped data is found by arranging the items in ascending or descending order of value, and selecting the item in the middle of the list.

Thus the median of seven values: 2, 4, 5, 6, 8, 9, 9 is equal to 6

and the median of six values: 1, 3, 3, 5, 6, 8 is equal to $\frac{3+5}{2} = 4$.

1.8 The median of a grouped frequency distribution can only be estimated approximately. The procedure is as follows.

(i) Establish the class to which the middle member belongs. This is called the *median class*. When calculating the median for grouped distributions, it is usual to take the middle member as $\frac{(n+1)}{2}$ for odd numbers, but $\left(\frac{n}{2}\right)$ for even numbers.

(ii)   A formula is then used to calculate the median.

> Median =   value of lower limit of median class + $(\dfrac{R}{f} \times c)$
>
> where R = difference between the middle member (ie $\dfrac{n+1}{2}$ or $\dfrac{n}{2}$) and the
>
> cumulative frequency up to the end of the preceding class
> f = frequency of median class
> c = width of median class

The median can also be found from an ogive; see question 17.

1.9   The geometric mean is sometimes used when one's main interest is in the percentage rate of change in a quantity. Some stock market indices use it. The geometric mean of $x_1, x_2, x_3 \ldots\ldots x_n$ is equal to

$$\sqrt[n]{x_1\ x_2\ x_3\ \ldots\ldots x_n}.$$

1.10   For example, the geometric mean of three values 1.5, 3 and 6 is equal to

$$\sqrt[3]{1.5 \times 3 \times 6}\ =\ \sqrt[3]{27}\ =\ 3$$

2.   Dispersion

2.1   Averages are a method of determining the 'location' or central point of a distribution, but they give no information about the shape of the frequency curve. Consider the frequency distributions of samples from two factories producing 15 centimetre diameter steel pipe:

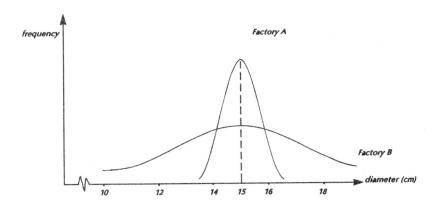

Both are spread evenly about the point representing 15cm, but Factory A obviously produces more accurate pipes than Factory B, even though the mean, median and mode of the two distributions are the same, ie 15cm. The differences between the distributions are caused by their 'spread' or dispersion. *Measures of dispersion* give some idea of the spread of a variable about its average.

113

2.2 One measure of dispersion is the range. It is the difference between the highest and lowest observations, so it gives an idea of the extreme values which might occur. The ranges from the graphs in paragraph 2.1 would be:

Factory A   13cm to 17cm = 4 centimetres
Factory B   10cm to 19cm = 9 centimetres

2.3 The complete range of a set of data may be rather unrepresentative of the dispersion of a frequency distribution because there may be a few values far away from all the other values. *Quartiles* are a means of identifying the range over which most of the frequencies in a distribution occur. A quartile is similar in concept to a median. There is an upper quartile and a lower quartile:

(i)   upper quartile: this is the value above which 25% of the observations fall;
(ii)   lower quartile: this is the value below which 25% of the observations fall.

50% of all observations therefore fall between the two quartiles.

2.4 A measure of dispersion in a frequency distribution is the quartile deviation. It is equal to half the difference between the two quartiles and is sometimes called the semi-inter-quartile range. The smaller the quartile deviation, the less spread out the distribution is.

2.5 The quartile coefficient of dispersion is another measure of dispersion using quartiles. It differs from the quartile deviation because it is expressed as a *proportion* and not in units of the variable. This is useful because it adjusts for the effect of the size of the data. The larger the values, the larger the difference between the quartiles, but $(Q_1 + Q_3)$ also grows with the values of the data, so dividing by $(Q_1 + Q_3)$ removes this effect. The lower the proportion, the less is the dispersion in the distribution.

$$\text{Quartile coefficient of dispersion} = \frac{Q_3 - Q_1}{Q_3 + Q_1}$$

where Q_1 is the lower quartile
Q_3 is the upper quartile

2.6 Another measure of dispersion is the mean deviation. This is the mean amount by which the values in a distribution differ from the arithmetic mean.

$$\text{Mean deviation} = \frac{\Sigma f|x - \bar{x}|}{n}$$

where $|x - \bar{x}|$ is the absolute difference between each value and the mean, ie the difference ignoring any minus sign

2.7 To calculate the mean deviation of grouped frequency distributions, remember to use the mid-point of the class intervals as the values for x.

2.8 The coefficient of mean deviation shows the size of the mean deviation relative to the size of the values of data. It is simply the mean deviation expressed as a proportion of the arithmetic mean:

$$\text{Coefficient of mean deviation} = \frac{\text{Mean deviation}}{\text{Arithmetic mean}}$$

2.9 The variance and the standard deviation are the two most widely used measures of dispersion mainly because they both lend themselves to further statistical analysis.

2.10 The variance is calculated as:

$$\text{Variance} = \sigma^2 = \frac{\Sigma f(x - \bar{x})^2}{\Sigma f}$$

Note that σ^2 denotes the variance. σ is the small Greek letter sigma. Σ is capital sigma.

2.11 The standard deviation is quite simply the (positive) square root of the variance:

$$\text{Standard deviation} = \sigma = \sqrt{\frac{\Sigma f(x - \bar{x})^2}{\Sigma f}}$$

Note that σ denotes the standard deviation.

2.12 The variance and standard deviation of a *sample* taken from a larger population are calculated in the same way. However the sample variance and standard deviation are denoted by s^2 and s respectively. The best estimates of the population standard deviation and the variance, given the sample data, are:

(a) $s^2 \times \left(\dfrac{n}{n-1} \right)$ for the population variance, where n is the number of items in the sample

(b) $s \times \sqrt{\dfrac{n}{n-1}}$ for the population standard deviation

The adjustment to s is known as 'Bessel's correction factor' and is valid for samples of any size. However, it is often ignored for large samples, because it is insignificant when n is large.

2.13 The *coefficient of variation*, sometimes known as the coefficient of relative dispersion, enables us to compare the dispersions of two distributions in different units, or where the magnitudes of the values are very different.

$$\text{Coefficient of variation} = \frac{\text{Standard deviation}}{\text{Arithmetic mean}}$$

The larger the coefficient of variation, the more widely dispersed is the frequency distribution.

2.14 You may need to determine the mean, variance and standard deviation of a number of items combined together. If so, the following rules apply:

Suppose there are three populations, P, Q and R, each with values independent of each other.

(i)   The mean of the population formed by combining items from the three populations is the sum of the individual population means $= \overline{x}(P) + \overline{x}(Q) + \overline{x}(R)$

(ii)   The variance of the population formed by combining items from the three populations is the sum of the individual population variances $= \sigma^2(P) + \sigma^2(Q) + \sigma^2(R)$

(iii)   Therefore the standard deviation of the population formed by combining items from the three populations

$$= \sqrt{\sigma^2(P) + \sigma^2(Q) + \sigma^2(R)}$$

For example, a product might comprise three components, each with their own distributions of weights, and we may want to know the mean and standard deviation of the weights of complete units.

3. Correlation and regression

3.1 Two variables may be linked in some way. There are two main questions we can ask.

(i)   How strong is the link? *Correlation coefficients* and the *coefficient of determination* answer this question.

(ii)   What exactly is the link? If the value of one variable increases by 1, we would like to know by how much the value of the other variable increases or decreases. We can compute a *regression line* to answer this question.

In answering either question, we will use a set of observations of pairs of values. We will observe the value of one variable (say x), and the corresponding value of the other (say y). We will call each pair of values of x and y a *data pair*. Our set of observations will comprise a number of data pairs.

3.2 The main correlation coefficient is the *Pearsonian correlation coefficient,* denoted by r. When people just refer to 'the correlation coefficient', they usually mean this one. It can take on values between +1 and -1. A value of +1 or -1 indicates *perfect correlation*, ie the link between the variables is as strong as it could be. Values nearer 0 indicate weaker links, and a value of 0 no link at all. Positive values of r indicate that as one variable rises, the other tends to rise (*positive correlation*). Negative values indicate that as one variable rises, the other tends to fall (*negative correlation*).

The formula for r is as follows.

For n data pairs,

$$r = \frac{n\Sigma xy - \Sigma x \Sigma y}{\sqrt{[n\Sigma x^2 - (\Sigma x)^2][n\Sigma y^2 - (\Sigma y)^2]}}$$

3.3 Because correlation is about how x and y vary together, there is a link with variance. As well as the variances of x and y, we can find the *covariance* of x and y, which is like the variance of one variable except that it takes account of both x and y.

Covariance of x and y

$$= \frac{\Sigma(x - \bar{x})(y - \bar{y})}{n}$$

We then have an alternative formula for r.

$$r = \frac{\text{Covariance of x and y}}{(\text{Standard deviation of x})(\text{Standard deviation of y})}$$

3.4 The *coefficient of determination* is r^2, the square of the Pearsonian correlation coefficient. This gives the proportion of the variation in one variable explained by variation in the other. It can take on values between 0 and 1. If its value is small, this suggests that we need to look for other explanations for the variation we are concerned with.

3.5 The other correlation coefficient is *Spearman's rank correlation coefficient,* denoted by r_s. It is used when the values of our variables are only ranks, or positions. for example, we might be given pairs of skaters' ranks, such as first (1) for technical merit and third (3) for artistic impression.

We compute r_s as follows.

For each of n pairs of ranks, compute the difference in ranks, d, ignoring minus signs (first-third = 1 - 3 = 2).

$$r_s = 1 - \frac{6\Sigma d^2}{n(n^2 - 1)}$$

Spearman's rank correlation coefficient can take on values from $+1$ to -1. As with the Pearsonian correlation coefficient, the nearer the coefficient is to $+1$ or -1, the stronger is the link between the two variables.

3.6 The exact nature of the link between two variables is shown by the *regression line*. Its full title is the *least squares linear regression line*. In order to find the equation of the line, we must decide which is the *independent variable* (ie the one which affects the other) and which is the *dependent variable* (ie the one which is affected by the other). The independent variable is usually denoted by x, and the dependent variable by y. The regression line is then called the regression line *of y on x*.

> For n data pairs, the least squares linear regression line is $y = a + bx$, where
>
> $$b = \frac{n\Sigma xy - \Sigma x \Sigma y}{n\Sigma x^2 - (\Sigma x)^2}$$
>
> $$a = \bar{y} - b\bar{x} = \frac{\Sigma y}{n} - \frac{b\Sigma x}{n}$$

a is a starting point, the value of y when $x = 0$. b shows how y changes as x changes. If b is positive, y rises as x rises. If b is negative, y falls as x rises. The larger the (positive or negative) value of b, the faster y changes as x changes.

3.7 Once we have worked out a regression line, we can take a value of x which we may not have observed, and put it into the equation $y = a + bx$, to work out the corresponding value of y. This is a prediction of the value of y for the given value of x.

3.8 There are some links between regression and correlation which can be handy in solving problems.

> In the regression line $y = a + bx$,
>
> $$b = \frac{\text{Covariance of x and y}}{\text{Variance of x}}$$

> If we have a regression line of y on x, $y = a + bx$, and one of x on y, $x = c + dy$, then we can find the Pearsonian correlation coefficient between x and y:
>
> $$r = \sqrt{bd}.$$
>
> Take the positive square root if b and d are positive, and the negative square root if they are negative.

QUESTIONS

1 The arithmetic mean of the five numbers 8, y, -15, -y and 22 is

A 3
B 5
C 9
D 15

Circle your answer

A   B   C   D

2 Sales of product P in May and June were 58 units and 48 units respectively. The arithmetic mean of monthly sales for the period January to April was 44 units per month.

The arithmetic mean of monthly sales for the period January to June is

A 39 units
B 40 units
C 47 units
D 50 units

Circle your answer

A   B   C   D

3 The arithmetic mean of the nine positive numbers 7, 2, q, 10, 3q, 8, q^2, 10 and 5 is equal to 7.

The value of q is

A 3
B 4
C 6
D 7

Circle your answer

A   B   C   D

4 A factory which employs 100 people is divided into three departments. The arithmetic mean output per employee per month for all employees is 139 units. Mean output per employee per month for two of the departments is as follows.

Department	No of employees in department	Mean output per employee per month units
1	54	130
2	22	160

What is the mean output per employee per month for department 3?

A   127 units
B   139 units
C   140 units
D   145 units

Circle your answer

A   B   C   D

5   The arithmetic mean of fifteen numbers is 20. When a sixteenth number, N, is added, the overall mean becomes 22. What is the value of N?

A   2
B   30
C   32
D   52

Circle your answer

A   B   C   D

6   A company budgets to achieve equal total sales revenues from each of its three products. The unit selling prices of the products are £15, £16 and £24 respectively.

What is the budgeted mean selling price per unit?

A   £15.85
B   £16.00
C   £17.56
D   £18.33

Circle your answer

A   B   C   D

7   A distribution manager has recorded the following daily distances travelled by vehicles in the department:

Distance travelled (miles) per day		Frequency
at least	less than	
0	5	5
5	10	10
10	20	8
20	30	2

What is the arithmetic mean distance travelled per day?

A   6.8 miles
B   9.5 miles
C   10.3 miles
D   13.8 miles

Circle your answer

A   B   C   D

8 A delivery vehicle makes a return journey between two depots which are 15 kilometres apart. The mean speed on the outward journey is 60 kilometres per hour (kph), but because of traffic congestion the mean speed on the inward journey is only 20 kph. What is the mean speed over the total return journey?

A   25 kph
B   30 kph
C   40 kph
D   45 kph

Circle your answer

A   B   C   D

9 A sales person travels between four customers who are situated equal distances apart. The journey between customers 1 and 2 is made at a speed of 30 kilometres per hour (kph), between customers 2 and 3 at 60 kph, and between customers 3 and 4 at 50 kph.

What was the mean speed travelled over the total of all journeys?

A   35.0 kph
B   42.9 kph
C   46.7 kph
D   57.1 kph

Circle your answer

A   B   C   D

10 The numbers of responses from nine different direct mail advertisements were as follows:

70, 70, 20, 60, 70, 20, 30, 40, 70

The median number of responses from an advertisement was

A   40
B   50
C   60
D   70

Circle your answer

A   B   C   D

11 The number of breakdowns last month of ten different machines was as follows:

3, 5, 11, 0, 8, 0, 3, 11, 0, 9

The median number of breakdowns was

A   0
B   4
C   5
D   8

Circle your answer

A   B   C   D

Data for questions 12 and 13

The number of jobs held by a group of young people since leaving school is as follows:

Number of jobs since leaving school	Frequency (number of people)
0	1
1	11
2	16
3	1
4	17
5	3
6	6

12 What is the median number of jobs held since leaving school?

A 2
B 3
C 4
D 6

Circle your answer

A	B	C	D

13 What is the mode of the number of jobs held since leaving school?

A 2
B 3
C 4
D 6

Circle your answer

A	B	C	D

14 In a retail outlet, the number of employees and the annual earnings per employee are as follows:

	Number employed	Annual earnings £
Manager	1	15,000
Supervisor	2	10,000
Administrator	3	12,000
Shelf filler	3	6,000
Storekeeper	2	11,000
Checkout operator	4	7,000

The median figure for annual earnings is

A   £6,000
B   £7,000
C   £9,000
D   £10,000

Circle your answer

A	B	C	D

Data for questions 15 and 16

An analysis of sales invoices outstanding at the end of February is as follows:

Invoice value		*Number of invoices*
at least £	*less than* £	
10	25	6
25	40	19
40	55	12
55	70	7
70	85	3

15 What is the approximate modal value of invoices outstanding at the end of February?

A   £32.50
B   £34.75
C   £39.21
D   £41.75

Circle your answer

A	B	C	D

16 What is the median value of invoices outstanding at the end of February?

A   £32.50
B   £34.75
C   £39.21
D   £41.75

Circle your answer

A	B	C	D

17 The following ogive shows the cumulative number of televisions in a town aged less than a certain number of years. The oldest television is twelve years old.

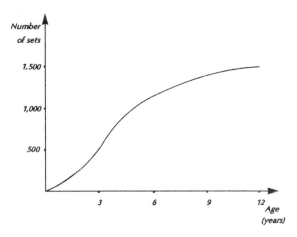

The median age of a television set in the town is approximately

A   3 years
B   4 years
C   6 years
D   7 years

Circle your answer

A   B   C   D

18 The following extract from a histogram shows the modal class and the two classes on either side of it.

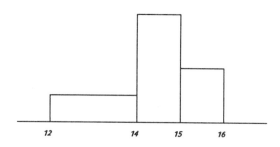

The approximate value of the mode is

A   14.125
B   14.375
C   14.625
D   14.875

Circle your answer

A   B   C   D

19 A share had a market price of £2.50 on 1 January. By 1 July, the share price had increased to £3.60. The geometric mean of the two share prices is

A   £2.47
B   £3.00
C   £3.05
D   £4.50

Circle your answer

A   B   C   D

20 The geometric mean of four positive numbers 8, 2p, 1, p is equal to 10.

The value of p is

A   2.5
B   10
C   25
D   625

Circle your answer

A   B   C   D

21 The geometric mean of two numbers is 10. When a third number N is included, the overall geometric mean remains unaltered at 10. What is the value of N?

A   0
B   1
C   10
D   900

Circle your answer

A   B   C   D

22 Consider the following statements about the frequency distribution shown below:

Statement

1. The lower quartile is 3
2. The median is 7
3. The upper quartile is 11

Frequency distribution

Value	Frequency
1	1
2	1
3	3
6	6
7	8
10	9
11	8
15	5
20	3

Which of the statements is/are correct?

A Statements 1 and 2 only
B Statements 1 and 3 only
C Statements 2 and 3 only
D Statement 3 only

Circle your answer

A	B	C	D

Data for questions 23 - 26

The following table shows the values of deliveries made to customers last week:

Value of delivery (£)		Frequency
at least	less than	
1	10	3
10	20	6
20	30	11
30	40	15
40	50	12
50	60	7
60	70	6

23 What is the value of the lower quartile in this frequency distribution?

A   £15.00
B   £20.00
C   £25.00
D   £25.45

Circle your answer

A   B   C   D

24 What is the value of the upper quartile, to the nearest £?

A   £40
B   £45
C   £48
D   £55

Circle your answer

A   B   C   D

25 What is the quartile deviation of the delivery values in the period, to the nearest £?

A   £11
B   £20
C   £23
D   £37

Circle your answer

A   B   C   D

26 What is the quartile coefficient of dispersion?

A   0.11
B   0.23
C   0.31
D   0.37

Circle your answer

A   B   C   D

Data for questions 27 and 28

The following frequency distribution shows the number of times that 80 machines have broken down in the last year:

Number of breakdowns in the year	Number of machines
6	8
7	12
8	20
9	22
10	16
11	2

27 What is the mean deviation of machine breakdowns in the year?

A   1.10 breakdowns
B   1.30 breakdowns
C   1.32 breakdowns
D   1.69 breakdowns

Circle your answer

A   B   C   D

28 What is the coefficient of mean deviation of this distribution?

A   0.13
B   0.15
C   0.16
D   0.18

Circle your answer

A   B   C   D

29 The following frequency distribution shows the range of stock values of 50 items:

Stock value held (£) at least	less than	Number of items
0	100	10
100	200	11
200	300	17
300	400	12

What is the mean deviation of the stock values held?

A £11.51
B £80.00
C £92.08
D £105.62

Circle your answer

A   B   C   D

30 What is the variance of the five numbers 4, 6, 8, 12, 15?

A 4
B 11
C 16
D 17

Circle your answer

A   B   C   D

31 A sample of seven out of two hundred children at a ballet school have the following ages:

4, 5, 6, 8, 10, 11, 12

What is the estimated standard deviation of the ages of the children at the ballet school (to 2 decimal places)?

A 2.88
B 3.11
C 8.29
D 9.67

Circle your answer

A   B   C   D

32 If a sample of n items is taken from a population, which of the following should be multiplied by the sample variance to estimate the population variance?

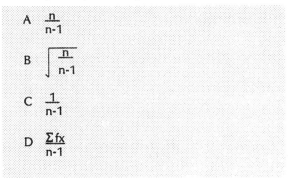

A $\dfrac{n}{n-1}$

B $\sqrt{\dfrac{n}{n-1}}$

C $\dfrac{1}{n-1}$

D $\dfrac{\Sigma fx}{n-1}$

Circle your answer

A   B   C   D

Data for questions 33 and 34

An auditor has selected the following sample of invoices (from a population of 8,000 invoices) for checking:

Value of invoice (£)		Number of invoices
at least	less than	
0	20	4
20	40	7
40	60	6
60	80	2
80	100	6

33 What is the arithmetic mean value of invoices selected?

A £49.20
B £51.25
C £56.00
D £70.00

Circle your answer

A	B	C	D

34 What is the estimated variance of the whole population of invoices?

A £27.99
B £28.57
C £783.36
D £816.00

Circle your answer

A	B	C	D

35 A statistician wishes to compare the dispersion of four frequency distributions. Data for the distributions are as follows:

Distribution	Mean	Standard deviation
1	£140	£33
2	£25,104	£6,290
3	77 kg	27 kg
4	154 miles	32 miles

The relative dispersion of the distributions is to be measured using the coefficient of variation. Which frequency distribution has the largest coefficient of variation?

A   Distribution 1
B   Distribution 2
C   Distribution 3
D   Distribution 4

Circle your answer

A   B   C   D

36 A large manufacturing company awards a 16% wage increase to every employee. Which of the following statements about the distribution of the company's wages is/are correct?

Statement
1.   The standard deviation will remain unaltered
2.   The standard deviation will increase by 16%
3.   The coefficient of variation will remain unaltered

A   Statement 1 only
B   Statement 2 only
C   Statements 1 and 3 only
D   Statements 2 and 3 only

Circle your answer

A   B   C   D

37 The demand per day for an item of stock has a mean of 26 units, with a standard deviation of 7.3 units. The demand on any day is unaffected by demand on any other day.

What is the standard deviation of the demand for a five day week?

A   7.3 units
B   16.3 units
C   36.5 units
D   37.2 units

Circle your answer

A   B   C   D

38 Three items X, Y and Z are sold together in a single packet. Their individual weights have the following means and standard deviations:

Product	Mean weight kg	Standard deviation kg
X	2	0.4
Y	1	0.1
Z	4	0.7

What is the standard deviation of the weight of a complete packet?

A   0.5 kg
B   0.7 kg
C   0.8 kg
D   1.2 kg

Circle your answer

A   B   C   D

39 The following four data pairs have been obtained.

x	y
4	12
3	15
1	10
3	14

What is the Pearsonian correlation coefficient between x and y?

A - 0.75
B - 0.55
C + 0.55
D + 0.75

Circle your answer

A   B   C   D

40 The Pearsonian correlation coefficient between two variables, x and y, is +0.72. What proportion of variation in x is explained by variation in y?

A 0.37
B 0.52
C 0.72
D 0.84

Circle your answer

A   B   C   D

41 Some data on values of x and y have been collected. The variance of the values of x is 42, and that of the values of y is 12. The covariance of the values of x and y is -20. What is the Pearsonian correlation coefficient between x and y?

A -0.2
B -0.79
C -0.89
D -0.94

Circle your answer

A   B   C   D

42 Five students each took two examinations, with the following results:

	Position	
Student	*First examination*	*Second examination*
P	1	5
Q	2	2
R	3	4
S	4	1
T	5	3

What is Spearman's rank correlation coefficient between the two sets of examination positions?

A - 0.25
B - 0.2
C + 0.2
D + 0.25

Circle your answer

A   B   C   D

43 What is the equation of the least-squares regression line for the following data pairs (x is the independent variable)?

x	y
0	3
1	4
2	6

A   y = 0.64 + 3.69x
B   y = 1.5 + 2.83x
C   y = 3.69 + 0.64x
D   y = 2.83 + 1.5x

Circle your answer

A   B   C   D

44 A regression line of y on x of y = -32 + 0.7x has been computed. What value of y would be predicted for a value of x of 48.5?

A   1.95
B   23.57
C   65.95
D   115

Circle your answer

A   B   C   D

45 A regression line of one variable, y, on another, x, is to be found. 20 data pairs have been obtained, and the following figures have been computed:

$\Sigma x = 210$ $\Sigma y = 500$ $\Sigma x^2 = 2{,}870$ $\Sigma xy = 6{,}580$

What is the value of a in the regression line y = a + bx?

A   -4
B   -2
C   +2
D   +4

Circle your answer

A   B   C   D

46 Two regression lines for the same set of data have been found, as follows:

$$y = 3.2 + 0.73x$$
$$x = -1.8 + 1.02y.$$

What is the coefficient of determination between the two variables, x and y?

A 0.55
B 0.74
C 0.86
D 0.88

Circle your answer

A   B   C   D

CHAPTER 8

INDEX NUMBERS. TIME SERIES ANALYSIS. NETWORKS

This chapter covers the following topics:

- Price indices and quantity indices
- Weighted indices of relatives
- Laspeyre and Paasche indices
- Time series analysis
- Networks

1. Price indices and quantity indices

1.1 An *index* measures changes in some variable over time. An *index number* is given to each time period (month, year, etc) to indicate the level of the variable for that time. Index numbers start at a *base period*, and an index number of 100 is assigned to that period. The difference between two values of an index for two different periods is called the number of *points* the index has risen or fallen. The plural of index is indices.

1.2 An index may be a price index or a quantity index.

(a) A *price index* measures changes in prices, either of one item or of a group of items. The Retail Prices Index (RPI), for example, measures changes in the total price of a selected 'basket' of items of consumer expenditure.

(b) A *quantity index* measures changes in variables other than prices. For example, a materials quantity index could measure changes in the quantity of materials used by a factory.

1.3 Where there is only one item for which an index is being worked out, the index for any given period is found as follows.

Price index	*Quantity index*
$\dfrac{p_1}{p_0} \times 100$	$\dfrac{q_1}{q_0} \times 100$
Where p_1 = price in the period under consideration p_0 = price in the base period	Where q_1 = quantity in the period under consideration q_0 = quantity in the base period

These indices measure prices and quantities in a period relative to those in the base period. For that reason, price indices of this sort are often called *price relatives* and quantity indices of this sort are often called *quantity relatives*.

2. Weighted indices of relatives

2.1 Most indices take account of changes in several items. One way of doing this is to compute a weighted average of the price relatives or quantity relatives of the individual items. Weights could be based on, for example, the proportions of total expenditure represented by the individual items in the base year.

2.2 For example, you might want to prepare a weighted index of price relatives for the current year for two items, bread and milk, from the following data.

	Price per unit		Weight
	Base year	*Current year*	
	pence	*pence*	
Bread	30	57	70%
Milk	16	24	30%

The index is computed as follows.

	Price relative		*Weight*		
Bread	57/30 = 1.9	×	70%	×100	133
Milk	24/16 = 1.5	×	30%	×100	45
					178

The index number for the current year is 178. This suggests that prices have risen on average by 78% since the base year, which would have had an index number of 100. However, we must be careful in interpreting index numbers, as different weights would give different numbers.

3. Laspeyre and Paasche indices

3.1 Rather than working out individual price or quantity relatives and then combining them in a weighted average, we can compile an index by going straight to the total price or quantity of a basket of items in the current year, and comparing that with the total price or quantity of the same basket in the base year. This is often felt to be a better approach. For example, an index to reflect changes in the cost of living should show the rise in the total cost of a household's typical weekly expenditure. Laspeyre and Paasche indices both use this approach of comparing whole baskets of items.

3.2 In a *Laspeyre price index*, the elements in the basket are weighted by base year quantities.

> Laspeyre price index $= \dfrac{\Sigma p_1 q_0}{\Sigma p_0 q_0} \times 100$
>
> where p_1 is the price of each item in the period under consideration
> p_0 is the price of each item in the base period
> q_0 is the quantity of each item consumed in the base period

3.3 An example will demonstrate how to use the formula for the Laspeyre price index.

A company uses two raw materials, M and N. Quantities used in year 1, together with the new material prices in years 1 and 5, are as follows:

Materials	Quantity used in year 1 (q_0) '000 kg	Price in year 1 (p_0) £ per kg	Price in year 5 (p_1) £ per kg	$p_1 q_0$ £'000	$p_0 q_0$ £'000
M	5	8	14.0	70	40
N	4	6	14.5	58	24
				128	64

Laspeyre price index for year 5 $= \dfrac{\Sigma p_1 q_0}{\Sigma p_0 q_0} \times 100 = \dfrac{128}{64} \times 100 = 200$

3.4 A *Laspeyre quantity or volume index* uses prices in the base year to weight the quantities:

> Laspeyre quantity or volume index $= \dfrac{\Sigma q_1 p_0}{\Sigma q_0 p_0} \times 100$
>
> where q_1 is the quantity of each item consumed in the period under consideration
> q_0 is the quantity of each item consumed in the base period
> p_0 is the price of each item in the base period

3.5 Laspeyre indices have the advantage that the bottom line, $\Sigma p_0 q_0$, remains the same from year to year. This means that any one period's index number can be validly compared with any other period's, and also that the work involved in compiling a series of index numbers is not too great. On the other hand, the weights (q_0 for price indices, p_0 for quantity indices) gradually get out of date.

3.6 An index in which the weightings are changed each period to reflect current conditions is called a *Paasche index*. The weights for a Paasche index are always up to date, but with such an index valid comparisons can only be made between the current period and the base period.

3.7 A *Paasche price index* uses quantities in the current period to weight the prices:

Paasche price index = $\dfrac{\Sigma p_1 q_1}{\Sigma p_0 q_1}$ x 100

where q_1 is the quantity of each item consumed in the period under consideration
p_1 is the price of each item in the period under consideration
p_0 is the price of each item in the base period

3.8 A *Paasche quantity* or *volume index* uses prices in the current period to weight the quantities:

Paasche quantity or volume index = $\dfrac{\Sigma q_1 p_1}{\Sigma q_0 p_1}$ x 100

where p_1 is the price of each item in the period under consideration
q_1 is the quantity of each item consumed in the period under consideration
q_0 is the quantity of each item consumed in the base period

---

4. Time series analysis

4.1 A time series is a series of figures or values recorded over time. Examples of time series are:

(i) output of a factory each day for the last month;
(ii) monthly sales over the last two years;
(iii) the Retail Prices Index each month for the last ten years.

4.2 A time series can be analysed into four components:

(i) *Trend* - the general long-term movement;
(ii) *Cyclical variations* - cycles over a long period, for example 10 years;
(iii) *Seasonal variations* - cycles over a shorter period, often a year but sometimes a month or some other period;
(iv) *Random variations* - these do not recur predictably.

4.3 In computational questions about time series, examiners usually concentrate on the trend, seasonal variations and random variations. They would have to give you a lot of data to bring in cyclical variations as well.

4.4 As an example of a time series, built up from a trend, seasonal variations and random variations, consider a company's sales figures over three years:

Year	Quarter	Trend	Seasonal variation	Random variation	Actual sales
		£	£	£	£
1	1	10,000	+1,000		11,000
	2	10,300	+300	+570	11,170
	3	10,600	-400		10,200
	4	10,900	-900		10,000
2	1	11,200	+1,000		12,200
	2	11,500	+300		11,800
	3	11,800	-400	+50	11,450
	4	12,100	-900		11,200
3	1	12,400	+1,000	-600	12,800
	2	12,700	+300		13,000
	3	13,000	-400		12,600
	4	13,300	-900		12,400

4.5 The point of this analysis is that we can predict future actual figures, by working out what the trend will be and making a seasonal adjustment.

In the above example, we can see that the trend figures increase by £300 each quarter. We could predict sales for year 4, quarter 2 as follows:

	£
Trend	13,900
Seasonal variation	300
Prediction	14,200

We could of course be wrong, because of unforeseen random variations, but we can reasonably hope not to be far wrong.

4.6 In the real world, we start with a series of actual figures, and have to discern the trend and seasonal variations from them. Your study text should, if time series analysis is within your syllabus, contain full worked examples of this. As a memory jogger, a short example involving six half-years is given here.

4.7 Example

Year	Half-year	Actual data	Two-halves totals	Four-halves totals	Trend	Seasonal variation
1	1	52				
			120			
	2	68		248	62	+6
			128			
2	1	60		272	68	-8
			144			
	2	84		308	77	+7
			164			
3	1	80		336	84	-4
			172			
	2	92				

The two-halves totals are free of seasonal variation, as each total comprises one first half-year and one second half-year. However, they hover between half-years (120, for example, is between the two halves of year 1), so we go on to add pairs of two-halves totals to get the four-halves totals, which line up with half-years. These are divided by 4 to get the trend (also called a moving average trend, because of how it is worked out), and our initial figure for the seasonal variation is the actual figure minus the trend figure.

4.8 We can go further, and get a completely regular seasonal variation, by averaging the seasonal variations we have found.

	Half-year		Total
	1	2	
Year 1		+6	
Year 2	-8	+7	
Year 3	-4		
	-12	+13	+1
Average	-6.00	+6.50	+0.5
Adjustment	-0.25	-0.25	-0.5
Adjusted average	-6.25	+6.25	0

An adjustment is made so that the seasonal variations total zero, so that they cancel out over a full year. The adjustment is spread evenly over the seasons.

4.9 We use our averaged seasonal adjustments in forecasting. Thus we could predict a value for year 4, half-year 1 as follows:

Prediction = predicted trend value + first half-year average seasonal variation.

From year 1, half-year 2 to year 3, half-year 1, a period of three half-years, the average trend increase each half-year was $\frac{84 - 62}{3} = 7.33$.

The predicted trend value for year 4, half-year 1 (two half-years on from year 3, half-year 1) is therefore 84 + 2 x 7.33 = 98.66. The prediction is therefore 98.66 - 6.25 = 92.41.

4.10 If we went back and combined our trend figures with our averaged seasonal variations for the periods for which we have actual data, we would reach figures slightly different from the actual data. For the first half-year of year 2, for example, 68 - 6.25 = 61.75, which exceeds the actual figure of 60 by 1.75.

These differences are called *residuals*. They may be due to random variations, or to the fact that seasonal variations do not in reality repeat exactly, but gradually change.

5. Networks

5.1 A *network* is a way of showing the *activities* needed to complete a project, and the order in which they must be done. Each activity is denoted by an *arrow*. All arrows start from and end at circles, called *nodes*. No activity starting at a node may be started until all activities ending at that node have been finished. Nodes commonly show a reference number, the *earliest time* by which all activities ending at the node could be completed and the *latest time* by which all activities ending at that node must be completed if the whole project is to be completed in the shortest possible time. A *path* through a network is any route from the start of the network to its end.

5.2 Example:

Activity	Preceded by	Duration days
A	-	14
B	-	5
C	B	7
D	A, C	2

The network is as follows:

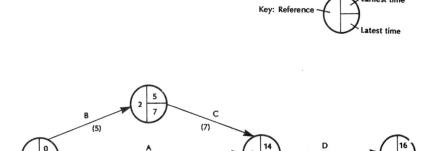

The paths through the network are AD and BCD.

Note that activity B could start two days late, or activity B could start on time but activity C could start two days late, and the whole project would still be completed on time. Activities A and D, on the other hand, must not be delayed at all; these activities constitute the *critical path*. The critical path is the path with the longest total duration. AD takes 14 + 2 = 16 days, while BCD takes 5 + 7 + 2 = 14 days

5.3 There may be several critical paths. Consider, for example, a project comprising just two activities, which may be carried on together and each of which takes 10 days. If either activity is delayed, the whole project is delayed, so each activity constitutes a critical path.

5.4 *Project evaluation and review technique* (PERT) deals with uncertainty in activity durations. When there is uncertainty, it is usual to assume that each uncertain activity duration is normally distributed, and that activity durations vary independently of one another. It is then possible to add the variances of durations of activities in a path through the network to get the variance of the duration of the whole path.

141

Usually, three durations are estimated for an activity, and the mean and standard deviation are estimated by conventional formulae.

o = optimistic duration
m = most likely duration
p = pessimistic duration

Estimated mean = $\dfrac{o + 4m + p}{6}$

Estimated standard deviation = $\dfrac{p - o}{6}$

QUESTIONS

Data for questions 1 and 2

An index of machine prices has year 1 as the base year, with an index number of 100. By the end of year 9 the index had risen to 180 and by the end of year 14 it had risen by another 18 points.

1 What was the percentage increase in machine prices between years 9 and 14?

A   2%
B   9%
C   10%
D   18%

Circle your answer

A   B   C   D

2 What was the average *annual* percentage price increase between years 9 and 14 (to one decimal place)?

A   1.8%
B   1.9%
C   2.0%
D   3.6%

Circle your answer

A   B   C   D

3 The price of a kilogram of raw material was £80 in year 1 and £120 in year 2. Using year 1 as a base year, the price index number for year 2 is

A   133
B   140
C   150
D   167

Circle your answer

A   B   C   D

4 A company used 20,000 litres of a raw material in year 1. In year 5 the usage of the same raw material amounted to 25,000 litres. Using year 1 as a base year, the quantity index number for year 5 is

A   105
B   120
C   125
D   180

Circle your answer

A   B   C   D

Data for questions 5 - 7

Constant Limited uses three grades of labour. The rates paid in years 1 and 4 and the average weekly labour hours in year 1 were as follows:

Grade of labour	Year 1 £ per hour	Year 4 £ per hour	Average weekly labour hours in year 1
Unskilled	2	2.32	180
Semi-skilled	3	3.60	140
Skilled	4	4.40	805

The company wishes to calculate a weighted index of price relatives for labour using year 1 as the base year. The weighting of the index is to be based on the proportions of total weekly wages incurred in year 1.

5 What percentage weighting will be applied to unskilled labour rates in the calculation of the index?

A   3.6%
B   9.0%
C   16.0%
D   22.2%

Circle your answer

A   B   C   D

6 What is the price relative of semi-skilled labour in year 4?

A   105
B   120
C   130
D   160

Circle your answer

A   B   C   D

7   What is the year 4 price index for labour, to the nearest whole number?

A   112
B   115
C   116
D   120

Circle your answer

A   B   C   D

8   A company wishes to construct a weighted index of price relatives for three commodities, L, M and N, using year 1 as a base year. Weights are to reflect total expenditure on each commodity in the base year. Relevant information is as follows:

Commodity	Year 1 quantity consumed in units	Year 1 price £ per unit	Year 3 price as a percentage of year 1 price %
L	4,000	2	102
M	8,000	5	90
N	4,000	8	98

The price index for year 3 will be

A   94.4
B   95.0
C   95.9
D   96.7

Circle your answer

A   B   C   D

9   Which of the following describes a Paasche price index?

A   An index in which the weightings are based on the prices in the base period

B   An index in which the weightings are based on the latest period's prices

C   An index in which the weightings are based on the quantities consumed in the base period

D   An index in which the weightings are based on the quantities consumed in the latest period

Circle your answer

A   B   C   D

Data for questions 10 and 11

A country uses three items as the basis for its wholesale price index. Relevant information about the items is as follows:

Item	Quantity purchased Year 1 '000 units	Price per unit Year 1 francs	Quantity purchased Year 6 '000 units	Price per unit Year 6 francs
X	50	10	80	30
Y	90	12	110	16
Z	110	14	130	12

Year 1 is used as the basis for all price indices.

10 What is the Laspeyre price index for year 6 (to 1 decimal place)?

A 136.5
B 145.2
C 183.3
D 211.5

Circle your answer

A   B   C   D

11 What is the Paasche price index for year 6 (to 1 decimal place)?

A 136.5
B 145.2
C 183.3
D 211.5

Circle your answer

A   B   C   D

Data for questions 12 - 15

A company has been in business for eight years, and now wishes to establish some indices to measure trends in its sales activity. Information concerning its three main products is as follows:

	Product F		Product G		Product H	
	Sales volume '000 units	Sales value £'000	Sales volume '000 units	Sales value £'000	Sales volume '000 units	Sales value £'000
Year 1	4.5	54.0	3.1	24.8	6.8	13.6
Year 8	6.8	95.2	4.1	45.1	8.6	60.2

The company intends to calculate all indices correct to one decimal place, using year 1 as the base year.

12 What is the Laspeyre price index for year 8?

A   152.4
B   156.6
C   230.4
D   237.1

Circle your answer

A   B   C   D

13 What is the Paasche price index for year 8?

A   152.4
B   156.6
C   230.4
D   237.1

Circle your answer

A   B   C   D

14 What is the Laspeyre volume index for year 8?

A   138.1
B   138.6
C   142.1
D   142.4

Circle your answer

A   B   C   D

15 What is the Paasche volume index for year 8?

A   138.1
B   138.6
C   142.1
D   142.4

Circle your answer

A   B   C   D

Data for questions 16 and 17

A company expresses the productivity in each of its two departments as a percentage, with 100% productivity representing standard productivity levels. The company now wishes to establish an annual index of productivity for both departments combined. The performance of each department is to be weighted to reflect the volume of output (in units) from the department.

Continued...

Data for year 1 and year 2 were as follows:

	Year 1		Year 2	
	Units of output per month	Productivity ratio	Units of output per month	Productivity ratio
Department	('000)	%	('000)	%
1	28	104	35	97
2	40	98	38	106

The productivity index is to be calculated to one decimal place, using year 1 as a base year.

16 The productivity index for year 2, using a Laspeyre index, will be

A 98.2
B 99.2
C 100.8
D 101.8

Circle your answer

A   B   C   D

17 The productivity index for year 2, using a Paasche index, will be

A 98.2
B 99.2
C 100.8
D 101.8

Circle your answer

A   B   C   D

18 A company maintains a price index for its major raw materials, which uses year 1 as base = 100. In year 12 the index for material R was 250 and the index for material S was 200.

Which of the following statements about year 12 can be deduced from this information?

Statement
1. The price per unit of material R is higher than the price per unit of material S.
2. The percentage change in the price of material R was 25% greater than the percentage change in the price of material S since year 1.
3. The percentage change in the price of material R was 50% greater than the percentage change in the price of material S since year 1.

A Statement 1 only
B Statement 2 only
C Statements 1 and 3 only
D Statement 3 only

Circle your answer

A   B   C   D

Data for questions 19 - 22

An extract from a country's retail prices index is as follows:

	Year 8	Year 9	Year 10
January	408.0	432.7	500.6
February		435.0	524.5
March		439.4	527.4
April		444.0	530.5

19 What was the percentage increase in prices between January year 10 and April year 10?

A 5.6%
B 6.0%
C 7.5%
D 29.9%

Circle your answer

A   B   C   D

20 What was the annual rate of inflation between February year 9 and February year 10?

A 17.1%
B 19.4%
C 20.6%
D 89.5%

Circle your answer

A   B   C   D

21 What was the average annual rate of inflation between January year 8 and January year 10?

A 9.3%
B 10.8%
C 11.4%
D 46.3%

Circle your answer

A   B   C   D

22 An item cost £5 in February year 9. Assuming that changes in the price of the item correspond exactly with changes in the Retail Prices Index, what was the price of the item in March year 10 (to the nearest penny)?

A   £4.12
B   £6.03
C   £6.06
D   £9.62

Circle your answer

A   B   C   D

23 A company's expenditure on stationery in July 1989 was £12,780. Prices of stationery are considered to change in line with the Retail Prices Index (RPI). The RPI for January 1988 was 103.3, and for July 1989 it was 115.5. What was the July 1989 expenditure on stationery, deflated to January 1988 prices?

A   £11,064
B   £11,221
C   £11,271
D   £11,430

Circle your answer

A   B   C   D

24 A company's expenditure on salaries was £227,900 in 19X3 and £298,150 in 19X6. An index of general salary levels was 129.3 in 19X3 and 152.7 in 19X6. What was the percentage increase in the company's expenditure on salaries in real terms over the period 19X3 to 19X6?

A   9.7%
B   10.8%
C   18.1%
D   30.8%

Circle your answer

A   B   C   D

25 Which of the following is *not* one of the four components of a time series?

A   Random variations
B   Cyclical variations
C   Four-quarter totals
D   Seasonal variations

Circle your answer

A   B   C   D

26 Which of the following components of a single time series would be identified as a cyclical variation?

A   A component increasing by the same amount each year over the last 50 years

B   Occasional peaks which occur unpredictably but on average once every five years

Continued...

C Regular cycles involving an increase in
   the first half of each year, followed by a
   corresponding decrease in the second half
   of the year

D A peak in the first three years of every
   decade, with a corresponding trough in
   the last five years of every decade

Circle your answer

| A | B | C | D |

27 In time series analysis, which of the following is true of seasonal variations?

A They always have a period of one year

B They always repeat exactly year after year

C They have a period shorter than that of
   any cyclical variations there may be

D If you combine the trend and the seasonal variations, you always get back to
   the actual data

Circle your answer

| A | B | C | D |

28 The following data are to be analysed into trend and seasonal variations. What is the seven-
day total for Friday of week 1?

Week	Day	Data
1	Monday	37
	Tuesday	44
	Wednesday	57
	Thursday	49
	Friday	51
	Saturday	38
	Sunday	42
2	Monday	50
	Tuesday	49
	Wednesday	56
	Thursday	44
	Friday	60
	Saturday	55
	Sunday	50

A 318
B 331
C 336
D 357

Circle your answer

| A | B | C | D |

29 The following data are to be analysed into trend and seasonal variations. What is the five-day average for Thursday of week 1?

Week	Day	Data
1	Monday	27
	Tuesday	29
	Wednesday	31
	Thursday	28
	Friday	26
2	Monday	30
	Tuesday	32
	Wednesday	35
	Thursday	34
	Friday	30

A 28
B 28.3
C 28.8
D 29

Circle your answer

A   B   C   D

Data for questions 30 and 31

Dairy sales for a retail outlet for three weeks are as follows:

	Sales units		
	Week 1	Week 2	Week 3
Monday	102	103	107
Tuesday	78	79	80
Wednesday	119	129	130
Thursday	92	95	95
Friday	99	100	107

The manager of the outlet wishes to analyse this time series of sales data.

30 What is the most appropriate moving average trend figure for Thursday of week 2?

A 94 units
B 101 units
C 102 units
D 108 units

Circle your answer

A   B   C   D

31 What is the average seasonal variation for Wednesday, to the nearest whole unit?

A   + 24 units
B   + 25 units
C   + 26 units
D   + 27 units

Circle your answer

A   B   C   D

Data for questions 32 and 33

Sales data for five quarters are as follows:

		Year 1			Year 2
Quarter	1	2	3	4	1
Sales units	76	90	92	64	80

---

32 For which quarter is it possible to calculate a trend figure?

A   Quarter 2, Year 1
B   Quarter 3, Year 1
C   Quarter 4, Year 1
D   Quarter 1, Year 2

Circle your answer

A   B   C   D

---

33 What is the trend figure for this quarter?

A   78.0 units
B   80.5 units
C   81.0 units
D   81.5 units

Circle your answer

A   B   C   D

---

34 A statistician is carrying out an analysis of a company's production output. The output varies according to the season of the year and from the available data she has calculated the following seasonal variations, in units of production:

	Spring	Summer	Autumn	Winter
Year 1			+ 11.2	+ 23.5
Year 2	-9.8	-28.1	+ 12.5	+ 23.7
Year 3	-7.4	-26.3	+ 11.7	

The average seasonal variation for autumn, to one decimal place, is

A   +11.7 units
B   +11.8 units
C   +11.9 units
D   +16.3 units

Circle your answer

A   B   C   D

Data for questions 35 - 37

A sales analyst has established the following trend figures and seasonal variations for a company's sales:

Quarter	1	2	3	4
	£'000	£'000	£'000	£'000
Year 7	1,500	1,528	1,552	1,530
Year 8	1,557	1,580	1,608	1,632
Average seasonal variation	-18	+3	+29	-14

The analyst forecasts that the trend will increase by £25,000 per quarter in years 9 and 10.

35 What is the forecast sales value for the third quarter of year 9 (in £'000)?

A   £1,678
B   £1,707
C   £1,736
D   £1,794

Circle your answer

A   B   C   D

36 What is the forecast sales value for the first quarter of year 10 (in £'000)?

A   £1,714
B   £1,739
C   £1,757
D   £1,775

Circle your answer

A   B   C   D

37 The actual sales achieved in the first quarter of year 9 amounted to £1,634,000. The residual for the quarter is

A + £23,000
B + £2,000
C -£5,000
D -£8,000

Circle your answer

A   B   C   D

38 In a network, activities are represented by arrows which start and end at circles called nodes. An activity starting at a node may begin when

A at least one of the activities ending at that node has been completed

B at least half of the activities ending at that node have been completed

C all activities on the critical path ending at that node have been completed

D all activities ending at that node have been completed

Circle your answer

A   B   C   D

39 Which of the following is true of critical paths through networks?

A They have greater durations than any non-critical paths through the same network.

B There is only one critical path through each network.

C Some networks have no critical paths.

D They contain more activities than any non-critical paths through the same network.

Circle your answer

A   B   C   D

40 The following activities comprise a project:

Activity	Preceded by	Duration (days)
E	-	8
F	-	3
G	F	2

Worker H performs activity E, and worker J performs activities F and G. The whole project is to be completed in the shortest possible time. Worker J starts work one day after worker H. How many days off may worker J take in between his two activities (assuming he takes no days off between starting and finishing one activity)?

A   0 days
B   1 days
C   2 days
D   3 days

Circle your answer

A   B   C   D

41 The following activities comprise a project:

Activity	Preceded by	Duration (days)
P	-	4
Q	-	7
R	Q	2
S	P	9
T	R, S	3

Within how many days could the whole project be completed?

A   12 days
B   14 days
C   16 days
D   19 days

Circle your answer

A   B   C   D

42 The following activities comprise a project:

Activity	Preceded by	Duration (days)
J	-	6
K	J	5
L	-	3
M	L	5
N	M, Q	4
P	L	2
Q	P	1

What is the critical path?

A   JK
B   LMN
C   LPQN
D   LMPN

Circle your answer

A   B   C   D

156

43 A path through a network comprises three activities of uncertain duration, as follows:

Activity	Preceded by	Duration (days)		
		Optimistic	Most likely	Pessimistic
X	-	2	3	4
Y	X	3	5	6
Z	Y	7	10	12

What is the probability that the whole path will be completed within 19 days?

Use the formulae for mean and standard deviation which are conventional in PERT.

A   0.4
B   0.6
C   0.8
D   0.9

Circle your answer

A   B   C   D

SECTION 2
MARKING SCHEDULES
AND COMMENTS

1: MARKING SCHEDULE

Question	Correct answer	Marks for correct answer	Question	Correct answer	Marks for correct answer	Question	Correct answer	Marks for correct answer
1	B	1	17	B	1	33	B	1
2	D	1	18	B	1	34	B	1
3	B	1	19	C	1	35	C	1
4	D	1	20	B	1	36	A	1
5	C	1	21	A	1	37	D	1
6	A	1	22	A	1	38	B	1
7	B	1	23	D	1	39	C	1
8	B	1	24	B	1	40	A	1
9	C	1	25	D	1	41	C	1
10	C	1	26	B	1	42	A	1
11	C	1	27	A	1	43	B	1
12	C	1	28	D	1	44	D	1
13	A	2	29	C	2	45	C	1
14	D	1	30	A	1	46	D	1
15	C	1	31	C	1			
16	B	1	32	C	2			

YOUR MARKS

Total marks available   49   Your total mark

1: MARKING SCHEDULE

GUIDELINES - If your mark was:

| 1 - 13 |
You need to do some thorough revision of basic algebra and mathematic principles. Go back to your study text and read the relevant sections, working carefully through all the examples.

| 26 - 37 |
Good, although there are probably still a few gaps in your knowledge. Even so, you are on the way to a good understanding of this topic.

| 14 - 25 |
You are still not sufficiently competent with basic algebra and mathematical principles. Read the comments on the solutions and then try this chapter again

| 38 - 49 |
Very good. You have got to grips with basic mathematical principles and you are ready to proceed with the remaining chapters in this book.

COMMENTS

Question

1

Figures within brackets should be worked out first, followed by multiplications and divisions. Additions and subtractions which are not bracketed should be done last.

Therefore $2 + 7 \times 5 - (-3 + 1) = 2 + 35 - (-2) = 39$

2

$-3 \times 4 + (-2 \times -1) - 7 \times (-2) + 3 \times 8$
$= -12 + 2 + 14 + 24$
$= 28$

3

$3^3 \times 2^3 + 5^2 \times 5^2 + 385^0$
$= 27 \times 8 + 5^4 + 1$
$= 216 + 625 + 1$
$= 842$

4

$x^8 \div x^4 = x^{(8-4)} = x^4$

5

When $x = 5$, $x^3 - 3x^2 + 22x - 156.5$
$\qquad = 5^3 - 3 \times 5^2 + 22 \times 5 - 156.5$
$\qquad = 125 - 75 + 110 - 156.5 = 3.5$

If $y^{\frac{1}{3}} = 3.5$,
$\quad y = (3.5)^3 = 42.875$

6

We first need to find the values of the three expressions which appear in the inequalities.

If $x = -3$ and $y = 2$, then

$-y^2 = -2^2 = -4$
$2xy = 2 \times -3 \times 2 = -12$
$x^3 = (-3)^3 = -27$

Since $-4 > -12 > -27$, A is the right answer.

Question

7
The negative in the index represents a 'reciprocal' or 'one over'.

Therefore x^{-3} is the reciprocal of, or one over, $x^3 = \dfrac{1}{x^3}$

8
When a number with an index is divided by the same number with an index, the second index is subtracted from the first index:

$$3^{-6} \div 3^{-2} = 3^{(-6-(-2))} = 3^{-4} = \dfrac{1}{3^4} = \dfrac{1}{81}$$

9
$\dfrac{27!}{24!3!}$ can be expressed as $\dfrac{27 \times 26 \times 25 \times 24!}{24! \times 3 \times 2 \times 1}$

Cancelling out the 24!, we have $\dfrac{27 \times 26 \times 25}{3 \times 2 \times 1} = 2{,}925$

10
$\dfrac{30!3!}{0!27!} = \dfrac{30 \times 29 \times 28 \times 3!}{0!} = \dfrac{30 \times 29 \times 28 \times 6}{1} = 146{,}160$

11
Since production increases by a constant amount each week, we have an arithmetic progression.

The nth term in an arithmetic progression is given by $a + (n - 1)d$, where:

a = production in week 1 ie 600
d = increase in production each week = 20
n = 15

$\therefore$ Production in week 10 = 600 + (15 - 1)20
= 880 units

12
The sum of the first n in terms of a series is given by:

$$S_n = \dfrac{n}{2}(a + z), \text{ where}$$

a = production in week 1, ie 600
z = production in last week, ie 880 (from previous question)

$\therefore$ Production in weeks 1-15

$= \dfrac{15}{2}(600 + 880)$

= 11,100

Question

13 Let the number of weeks required to complete the order be n.

$$S_n = \frac{n}{2}(a + z) \text{ where}$$

$$S_n = 228{,}000$$
$$a = 7{,}200$$
$$d = 200$$
$$z = a + (n - 1)d$$

$$\therefore \quad 228{,}000 = \frac{n}{2}(7{,}200 + (7{,}200 + (n - 1)\,200))$$

$$= \frac{n}{2}(14{,}400 + 200n - 200)$$

$$\therefore \quad 228{,}000 = 100n^2 + 7{,}100n$$
$$0 = 100n^2 + 7{,}100n - 228{,}000$$
$$0 = n^2 + 71n - 2{,}280$$

Solving the quadratic equation we get:

$$n = \frac{-b \pm \sqrt{b^2 - 4ac}}{2a}$$

$$= \frac{-71 \pm \sqrt{(71)^2 - 4 \times 1 \times (-2{,}280)}}{2}$$

$$= \frac{-71 \pm \sqrt{5{,}041 + 9{,}120}}{2}$$

$$= \frac{-71 + 119}{2} \text{ or } \frac{-71 - 119}{2}$$

$$= 24 \text{ or } -95$$

Since we cannot have a negative solution, the time to complete the order is 24 weeks.

14 Output in the 8th week $= a + (n - 1)d$ where
$$a = 7{,}200$$
$$n = 8$$
$$d = 200$$
$$= 7{,}200 + (8 - 1)\,200$$
$$= 8{,}600 \text{ units}$$

Total output in first 8 weeks $= \frac{n}{2}(a + z)$ where

$$n = 8$$
$$a = 7{,}200$$
$$z = 8{,}600$$

Continued...

Question

Total output in first 8 weeks $= \dfrac{8}{2}(7{,}200 + 8{,}600)$

$= 63{,}200$ units

∴ Units required to complete the order
after 8 weeks $= 228{,}000 - 63{,}200 = 164{,}800$ units

∴ Weeks to complete the order
after 8 weeks
$= 164{,}800 \div 8{,}600$ units per week
$= 19$ weeks, to the nearest week

∴ Total time to complete order $= (19 + 8)$ weeks
$= 27$ weeks

15 The nth term in a geometric progression is: $ar^{(n-1)}$

The 12th term is therefore $\quad ar^{(12-1)}$
where a is year 1 sales $\quad = 6{,}750$
$\quad$ r is rate of growth $\quad = 1.2$ or 120%
∴ Sales in year 12 $\quad = 6{,}750 \times 1.20^{11}$
$\quad = 50{,}153$ units

16 If the third term of the progression is 18, and the common ratio is 3, then the first term must be $18 \div 3 \div 3 = 2$.

The sum of the first five terms is given by $\quad \dfrac{a(1 - r^5)}{1 - r}$

where $\quad a = $ first term $= 2$
$\quad r = 3$

∴ Sum of first five terms $\quad = \dfrac{2(1 - 3^5)}{1 - 3} = \dfrac{2(1 - 243)}{-2} = 242$

17 Sales are reduced by a constant proportion (0.5); therefore this is a geometric progression.

$a = 2{,}048$
$n = 9$
$r = 0.5$

$S_n = 2{,}048 \dfrac{0.5^9 - 1}{0.5} = 4{,}088$

Question

18 Sales of Reds are also in the form of a geometric progression. October is the 10th term in the progression.

The 10th term is given by $ar^{(10-1)}$

$$\text{where} \quad a \quad = \quad 1,000$$
$$r \quad = \quad 1.20$$
$$\therefore \text{Sales in October} \quad = \quad 1,000 \times (1.20)^9$$
$$= \quad 5,160 \text{ units}$$

19 The sum of the first 12 terms of this geometric progression is:

$$S_n \quad = \quad \frac{a\,(1 - r^{12})}{1 - r}$$

$$\text{Where} \quad a \quad = \quad 1,000$$
$$r \quad = \quad 1.20$$

$$\therefore \text{Sales next year} \quad = \quad \frac{1,000\,(1 - 1.20^{12})}{1 - 1.20}$$

$$= \quad \frac{1,000\,(1 - 8.92)}{1 - 1.20}$$

$$= \quad 39,600 \text{ units}$$

20 Let X, Y, Z be the number of housewives purchasing a single product, and let XY, YZ, XZ be the number of housewives purchasing two products.

$$Y \quad = \quad 177 \quad (1)$$
$$XY \quad = \quad 36 \quad (2)$$
$$X + Y + XY \quad = \quad 441 \quad (3)$$
$$X + Y \quad = \quad 405 \quad (3) - (2) = (4)$$
$$X \quad = \quad 228 \quad (4) - (1)$$

21 Using the same notation as in the previous question:

$$Y \quad = \quad 177$$
$$Z \quad = \quad 111$$
$$Y + Z + YZ \quad = \quad 306$$
$$YZ \quad = \quad 306 - 111 - 177$$
$$= \quad 18$$

Question

22 Using the same notation as in the previous two questions, and the solutions to those questions:

Number of housewives who have made a purchase $= X + Y + Z + XY + XZ + YZ$
$= 228 + 177 + 111 + 36 + 42 + 18$
$= 612$

Total interviewed $= 750$

Number of housewives who have
never purchased X, Y or Z $= 750 - 612 = 138$

23 The terms in the equation can be re-arranged step by step:

$$F = \frac{5yz}{v(x-2)}$$

$$Fv(x-2) = 5yz$$

$$x - 2 = \frac{5yz}{Fv}$$

$$x = \left(\frac{5yz}{Fv}\right) + 2$$

24 Each unit made and sold brings in sales revenue of £8.50, but costs £3 to make. By making and selling one extra unit, the company is therefore £8.50 - £3 = £5.50 better off.

At zero production, the company makes a loss equal to its fixed costs of £5,000. It must make enough units to cover these costs, in order to work up to a position of no loss and no profit.

Number of units x £5.50 = £5,000

Number of units = £5,000/£5.50 = 909.

25 To make a profit of £8,300, the company must first make and sell enough units to cover the fixed costs, and then work up to this profit.

Number of units x £5.50 $= £5,000 + £8,300 = £13,300$

Number of units $= £13,300/£5.50 = 2,418$

Question

26

$$3x - 2y = 30 \quad (1)$$
$$4x + 3y = 57 \quad (2)$$

(1) x 4 $\quad 12x - 8y = 120 \quad (3)$
(2) x 3 $\quad 12x + 9y = 171 \quad (4)$
(3) - (4) $\quad - 17y = -51$
$$y = 3$$

Substitute in (1)

$$3x - 6 = 30$$
$$3x = 36$$
$$x = 12$$

27

$$5y = 3x - 16 \quad (1)$$
$$2y = 4x + 2 \quad (2)$$

(1) x 2 $\quad 10y = 6x - 32 \quad (3)$
(2) x 5 $\quad 10y = 20x + 10 \quad (4)$
(3) - (4) $\quad 0 = -14x - 42$
$$14x = -42$$
$$x = -3$$

Substitute in (1)

$$5y = -9-16 = -25$$
$$y = -5$$

28 Substitute the pairs of values for P and Q in the equation:

$$14 = x + 17y \quad (1)$$
$$20 = x + 14y$$

Subtract $\quad -6 = 3y$
$$y = -2$$

Substitute in (1)

$$14 = x - 34$$
$$x = 14 + 34$$
$$= 48$$

29

$$p + 2q - r = 12 \quad (1)$$
$$p + q + 2r = 5 \quad (2)$$
$$3p - q + r = 4 \quad (3)$$

From (1), $\qquad\qquad r = p + 2q - 12$

Continued...

169

Question

Substitute in (2) and (3):

In (2) $p + q + 2(p + 2q - 12)$ = 5
                              $3p + 5q$ = 29   (4)
In (3) $3p - q + p + 2q - 12$ = 4
                              $4p + q$ = 16   (5)

Multiply (5) by 5 $20p + 5q$ = 80   (6)
(6) - (4) $17p$ = 51
                              p = 3

Substitute in (4) $3(3) + 5q$ = 29
                              $5q$ = 20
                              q = 4

30   First, multiply out the brackets:

$$(x - 8) \ (x - 3) = 2 + 2x$$
$$x^2 - 3x - 8x + 24 = 2 + 2x$$
$$x^2 - 13x + 22 = 0$$

Factorise, $(x - 11) \ (x - 2) = 0$

Therefore, $x = 11$ or $x = 2$

31   Two methods which you could have used to solve this question are:

(a)   factorise the expression yourself, and then select the option which corresponds to your answer; or

(b)   multiply out the brackets for each option until you find the one which gives the correct result.

32   First, factorise the equations:

$$x^2 + 5xy + 4y^2 = 55$$
$$(x + 4y) \ (x + y) = 55 \quad (1)$$
$$x^2 + 7xy + 12y^2 = 99$$
$$(x + 4y) \ (x + 3y) = 99 \quad (2)$$

Divide (2) by (1)
$$\frac{(x + 3y)}{(x + y)} = \frac{9}{5}$$

Cross multiply
$$5x + 15y = 9x + 9y$$
$$6y = 4x$$
$$x = 1.5y \quad (3)$$

Continued...

Question

Substitute in equation (1)

$$(1.5y + 4y) \; (1.5y + y) = 55$$
$$(5.5y) \; (2.5y) = 55$$
$$13.75y^2 = 55$$
$$y^2 = 4$$
$$y = \pm 2$$

Substituting $y = 2$ in equation (3) we get

$$x = 3$$

Substituting $y = -2$ in equation (3) we get

$$x = -3$$

33 For a value for y of 4, $\quad 3x^2 + 8x - 7 = 4$
$$\therefore 3x^2 + 8x - 11 = 0$$

$$\text{Using } x = \frac{-b \pm \sqrt{b^2 - 4ac}}{2a}$$

$$x = \frac{-8 \pm \sqrt{64 - (4)(-11)(3)}}{6}$$

$$= \frac{-8 \pm \sqrt{64 + 132}}{6}$$

$$= \frac{-8 \pm 14}{6} = -\frac{22}{6} \text{ or } \frac{6}{6}$$

Therefore, $x = -3\frac{2}{3}$ or $x = 1$.

34 The total number of deliveries this month will be $1,500 + 750 = 2,250$.

Let the required percentage be x.

$$(750x) + (1,500 \times 88) = 2,250 \times 90$$
$$750x = 202,500 - 132,000$$
$$= 70,500$$
$$x = 94$$

$\therefore$ 94% of the deliveries for the remainder of the month must be same-day.

Question

35 We must first get both equations into a form with terms including x or y on the left, and numbers not involving x or y on the right.

$$y = 7x - 4$$
$$\text{becomes } -7x + y = -4$$

$$3x = 2y + 9$$
$$\text{becomes } 3x - 2y = 9$$

The first row of the square matrix is -7 1. and the second row is 3 -2. The column matrix on the right has -4 at the top, and 9 below.

The answer is

$$\begin{pmatrix} -7 & 1 \\ 3 & -2 \end{pmatrix} \begin{pmatrix} x \\ y \end{pmatrix} = \begin{pmatrix} -4 \\ 9 \end{pmatrix}$$

36
$$\begin{pmatrix} 3 & 2 \\ 4 & 7 \end{pmatrix} \begin{pmatrix} 1 & -3 \\ 0.5 & -2 \end{pmatrix} = \begin{pmatrix} 3 \times 1 + 2 \times 0.5 & 3 \times -3 + 2 \times -2 \\ 4 \times 1 + 7 \times 0.5 & 4 \times -3 + 7 \times -2 \end{pmatrix}$$

$$= \begin{pmatrix} 4 & -13 \\ 7.5 & -26 \end{pmatrix}$$

37
$$\begin{pmatrix} 2 & 0 & -3 \\ -1 & 7 & 0 \end{pmatrix} \begin{pmatrix} 1 & 9 \\ 2 & -5 \\ -4 & 3 \end{pmatrix} = \begin{pmatrix} 2 \times 1 + 0 \times 2 - 3 \times -4 & 2 \times 9 + 0 \times -5 - 3 \times 3 \\ -1 \times 1 + 7 \times 2 + 0 \times -4 & -1 \times 9 + 7 \times -5 + 0 \times 3 \end{pmatrix}$$

$$= \begin{pmatrix} 14 & 9 \\ 13 & -44 \end{pmatrix}$$

38
$$\begin{pmatrix} 4 & 1 \\ 8 & 3 \end{pmatrix}^{-1} = \frac{1}{4 \times 3 - 1 \times 8} \begin{pmatrix} 3 & -1 \\ -8 & 4 \end{pmatrix} = \frac{1}{4} \begin{pmatrix} 3 & -1 \\ -8 & 4 \end{pmatrix} = \begin{pmatrix} 0.75 & -0.25 \\ -2 & 1 \end{pmatrix}$$

39 An identity matrix is one with 1's in the diagonal from top left to bottom right, and 0's everywhere else.

Question

40

The first step is to calculate the contribution per unit for each product:

Product X contribution = £15 - £13 = £2 per unit
Product Y contribution = £41 - £38 = £3 per unit

With constant fixed costs, profit is maximised when contribution is maximised. This occurs at vertex number 2:

Maximum contribution	= (2,400 x £2) + (1,200 x £3)
	= 8,400
less fixed costs	5,200
Maximum monthly profit	3,200

42

The constraint on the maximum availability of semi-skilled labour is;

$$2P + 6Q + 12R \leqslant 7,000$$

which can be simplified to

$$P + 3Q + 6R \leqslant 3,500$$

43

The constraint on the minimum amount of skilled labour to be used is

$$6P + 8Q + 4R \geqslant 4,000$$

This can be simplified to

$$3P + 4Q + 2R \geqslant 2,000$$

44

The constraint on the required proportion of sales of product P is

$$P \geqslant 0.2 (P + Q + R)$$

To simplify, multiply by 5

$$5P \geqslant P + Q + R$$
$$\therefore \quad 4P - Q - R \geqslant 0$$

Question

45 The constraint F $\leq$ 2 is plotted as a straight line parallel to the horizontal axis, at the point where F = 2. This restricts our choice to graphs 1, 2 or 3.

The easiest points to plot for the constraint 3E + 4F $\leq$ 36 are those when:

(a) E = 0, 4F = 36 $\therefore$ F = 9
(b) F = 0, 3E = 36 $\therefore$ E = 12

Considering graphs 1, 2 and 3 only, this constraint is correctly drawn in Graphs 2 and 3.

Since F must be *less* than or equal to 2, the feasible area must lie *underneath* the F = 2 line, therefore the correct area is shaded in Graph 3.

46 An iso-contribution line joins points on a graph which earn the same total contribution. If we calculate the contributions at the points where each of the graphs cut the axes, we find that the only line which joins points of equal contribution is graph 4:

When M = 0, 3 x L @ £4 = £12 contribution
When L = 0, 4 x M @ £3 = £12 contribution

2: MARKING SCHEDULE

Question	Correct answer	Marks for correct answer	Question	Correct answer	Marks for correct answer	Question	Correct answer	Marks for correct answer
1	B	1	10	C	1	19	D	1
2	A	1	11	A	2	20	A	2
3	A	1	12	B	1	21	B	1
4	C	2	13	C	1	22	D	1
5	C	2	14	C	1	23	D	1
6	B	2	15	A	1	24	D	1
7	A	1	16	B	1	25	C	1
8	B	1	17	A	1	26	B	1
9	A	1	18	B	1	27	B	1

YOUR MARKS

Total marks available   32   Your total mark

GUIDELINES - If your mark was:

0 - 9

Poor. You do not understand many of the basic principles of calculus. Go back to your study text and work though each relevant section carefully, then have another attempt at the questions in this chapter.

17 - 25

Good. You are still making a few errors, but you are getting there!

10 - 16

Fair. You are still being caught out by some of the more tricky data manipulations. Think carefully about the reasons for your errors and then try the chapter again.

26 - 32

Very good. You have a sound understanding of the principles of calculus which gives you a good grounding for the rest of your studies.

COMMENTS

Question

1

$$y = 4x^3 + 2x^2 + 7x - 9$$

$$\frac{dy}{dx} = 12x^2 + 4x + 7$$

When x = 4,

$$\frac{dy}{dx} = 12(4)^2 + 4(4) + 7 = 215$$

2

$y = 7x^2 + x - 6$. The gradient of the curve at any point is given by $\frac{dy}{dx}$.

$$\frac{dy}{dx} = 14x + 1$$

When x = -3,

$$\frac{dy}{dx} = 14(-3) + 1 = -41$$

3

$$2s = 3t^2 - 4t + 6$$

$$s = \frac{3}{2}t^2 - 2t + 3$$

$$\frac{ds}{dt} = 3t - 2$$

When t = 5,

$$\frac{ds}{dt} = 15 - 2 = 13$$

4

$$y = \frac{14}{x} - \frac{2}{x^2}$$

$$= 14x^{-1} - 2x^{-2}$$

$$\frac{dy}{dx} = -14x^{-2} + 4x^{-3}$$

$$= \frac{-14}{x^2} + \frac{4}{x^3}$$

Question

5

$$p = \sqrt{q} - \frac{1}{q} + \frac{q}{2}$$

$$p = q^{\frac{1}{2}} - q^{-1} + \frac{q}{2}$$

$$\frac{dp}{dq} = \frac{1}{2}q^{-\frac{1}{2}} + q^{-2} + \frac{1}{2}$$

$$= \frac{1}{2\sqrt{q}} + \frac{1}{q^2} + \frac{1}{2}$$

When q = 4

$$\frac{dp}{dq} = \frac{1}{2\sqrt{4}} + \frac{1}{4^2} + \frac{1}{2}$$

$$= \frac{1}{4} + \frac{1}{16} + \frac{1}{2} = \frac{13}{16}$$

6

$$u = 4\sqrt{v} - \frac{1}{v^3}$$

$$= 4v^{\frac{1}{2}} - v^{-3}$$

$$\frac{du}{dv} = 2v^{-\frac{1}{2}} + 3v^{-4}$$

$$= \frac{2}{\sqrt{v}} + \frac{3}{v^4}$$

7

$$C = 16 + Q + 3Q^2$$

The marginal cost function can be found by differentiating this total cost function:

$$\frac{dC}{dQ} = 1 + 6Q$$

When Q = 8, marginal cost, $\frac{dC}{dQ} = 1 + (6 \times 8) = £49$

177

Question

8

$$P = 8 - 0.05Q$$

Since revenue, R = Quantity x Price = Q x P
$$R = Q(8 - 0.05Q)$$
$$= 8Q - 0.05Q^2$$

Marginal revenue, $\dfrac{dR}{dQ}$ = $8 - 0.1Q$

$$C = 400 + 5Q + 0.1Q^2$$

Marginal cost, $\dfrac{dC}{dQ}$ = $5 + 0.2Q$

To maximise profit, marginal cost = marginal revenue

$$5 + 0.2Q = 8 - 0.1Q$$
$$0.3Q = 3$$
$$Q = 10$$

The quantity of sales to maximise profit is therefore 10,000 units

9

$$c = 3v^2 - 180v - 70$$

$$\dfrac{dc}{dv} = 6v - 180$$

Average cost is at a minimum when

$$\dfrac{dc}{dv} = 0 \text{ and } \dfrac{d^2c}{dv^2} > 0$$

When $6v - 180 = 0$
$$6v = 180$$
$$v = 30$$

$$\dfrac{d^2c}{dv^2} = 6$$

As this is greater than 0, $v = 30$ is a minimum.

The average unit cost will therefore be lowest when the volume of production is equal to 30 units.

Question

10

We need to find an expression for total revenue in terms of price, and then differentiate that function.

$$\text{Let } R = \text{total revenue}$$
$$R = Dp = (35p + 7,000 - 7p^2)p$$
$$R = 35p^2 + 7,000p - 7p^3$$

$$\frac{dR}{dp} = 70p + 7,000 - 21p^2$$

At maximum total revenue, $\frac{dR}{dp} = 0$.

11

$$y = 210x - 5x^2$$

$$\frac{dy}{dx} = 210 - 10x$$

There is a maximum or minimum where

$$\frac{dy}{dx} = 210 - 10x = 0$$

$$210 = 10x$$
$$x = 21$$

At this point $\frac{d^2y}{dx^2} = -10$ which is < 0.

Therefore y is at maximum when $x = 21$.

The graph of y cuts the x axis when

$$y = 0$$
$$\text{ie where } 210x - 5x^2 = 0$$
$$5x(42-x) = 0$$

which occurs both at $x = 0$ and at $x = \frac{210}{5} = 42$.

Therefore statement 1 is the only one which is true.

Question

12

$$y = x^3 - 9x^2 + 24x - 4$$

$$\frac{dy}{dx} = 3x^2 - 18x + 24$$

y is at a minimum or maximum when $3x^2 - 18x + 24 = 0$, which can be factorised as

$$(3x - 12)\ (x - 2) = 0$$

Either $(3x - 12) = 0$

$x = 4$

Or $(x - 2) = 0$

$x = 2$

$$\frac{d^2y}{dx^2} = 6x - 18$$

When x = 4, $\frac{d^2y}{dx^2} = 24 - 18 = 6$. This is positive, therefore we have a minimum point when x = 4.

When x = 2, $\frac{d^2y}{dx^2} = 12 - 18 = -6$. This is negative, therefore we have a maximum point when x = 2.

13

$$y = x^3 - 4x^2 - 11x + 6$$

$$\frac{dy}{dx} = 3x^2 - 8x - 11$$

y is at a minimum or maximum when $3x^2 - 8x - 11 = 0$

Solving, using $x = \dfrac{-b \pm \sqrt{b^2 - 4ac}}{2a}$

$$x = \frac{8 \pm \sqrt{64 - 4(3)(-11)}}{6}$$

$$= \frac{8 \pm \sqrt{196}}{6}$$

$$= \frac{8 + 14}{6} \text{ or } \frac{8 - 14}{6}$$

$$= 3\tfrac{2}{3} \text{ or } -1$$

$$\frac{d^2y}{dx^2} = 6x - 8$$

Continued...

Question

When $x = 3\frac{2}{3}$, $\dfrac{d^2y}{dx^2} = (3\frac{2}{3} \times 6) - 8$

$= 22 - 8$

$= 14$

This is positive, therefore y is at a minimum when $x = 3\frac{2}{3}$.

14

$$r = 6.5q^2 - q^3 + 10q$$

$$\frac{dr}{dq} = 13q - 3q^2 + 10$$

$$= -3q^2 + 13q + 10$$

This is a maximum or minimum point when $-3q^2 + 13q + 10 = 0$

Solving, using $q = \dfrac{-b \pm \sqrt{b^2 - 4ac}}{2a}$

$$q = \frac{-13 \pm \sqrt{169 - 4(-3)(10)}}{-6}$$

$$= \frac{-13 \pm 17}{-6}$$

$$= -\tfrac{2}{3} \text{ or } 5$$

Since output cannot be negative, we have a maximum or minimum point where $q = 5$.

$$\frac{d^2r}{dq^2} = -6q + 13$$

When $q = 5$, $\dfrac{d^2r}{dq^2} = -30 + 13 = -17$. This is a negative number, therefore r is at a maximum when $q = 5$.

15

$$c = q^2 - 1.25q + 30$$

Marginal cost $= \dfrac{dc}{dq} = 2q - 1.25$

When $q = 4.8$, (q is quantity *in thousands*)

$= (2 \times 4.8) - 1.25$

$= £8.35$

Question

16 We can use the economic theory that profit is maximised when marginal cost is equal to marginal revenue.

Marginal revenue $= \dfrac{dr}{dq} = 13q - 3q^2 + 10$ (from question 14)

Marginal cost $= \dfrac{dc}{dq} = 2q - 1.25$ (from question 15)

$\therefore$ Therefore profit is maximised when $13q - 3q^2 + 10 = 2q - 1.25$

Rearranging, $\quad 3q^2 - 11q - 11.25 = 0$

Solve, using $q = \dfrac{-b \pm \sqrt{b^2 - 4ac}}{2a}$

$= \dfrac{11 \pm \sqrt{121 - 4(3)(-11.25)}}{6}$

$= \dfrac{11 \pm \sqrt{256}}{6}$

$= \dfrac{27}{6}$ or $\dfrac{-5}{6}$

Since output cannot be negative, we have maximum profit where $q = \dfrac{27}{6} = 4.5$

Profit is maximised when output is 4,500 units.

17 $\displaystyle\int_0^2 3x^3 dx = \left[\dfrac{3x^4}{4} \right]_0^2 = \tfrac{3}{4} \times 2^4 = \tfrac{3}{4} \times 16 = 12.$

18 $\displaystyle\int_0^3 (6q^2 + 4q - 7)dq$

$= \left[\dfrac{6q^3}{3} + \dfrac{4q^2}{2} - 7q \right]_0^3$

$= \left[2q^3 + 2q^2 - 7q \right]_0^3$

$= 54 + 18 - 21 = 51$

Question

19

$$\int_3^6 (4q - 1)dq = \left[\frac{4q^2}{2} - q \right]_3^6$$

$$= [\, 2q^2 - q \,]_3^6$$

$$= (2(36) - 6) - (2(9) - 3) = 51$$

20

$$\int_1^2 \left(3v - \frac{2}{v^2} + 0.25\right) dv = \int_1^2 (3v - 2v^{-2} + 0.25)dv$$

$$= \left[\frac{3v^2}{2} + \frac{-2}{-2+1} \, v^{-2+1} + 0.25v \right]_1^2$$

$$= \left[\frac{3v^2}{2} + 2v^{-1} + 0.25v \right]_1^2$$

$$= \left[\frac{3v^2}{2} + \frac{2}{v} + 0.25v \right]_1^2$$

$$= \frac{3}{2}(4) + \frac{2}{2} + 0.25(2) - \left(\frac{3}{2}(1) + \frac{2}{1} + 0.25(1)\right)$$

$$= 6 + 1 + 0.5 - (1.5 + 2 + 0.25) = 3.75$$

21

The *marginal* cost of production is the rate of change of cost of production, therefore

total cost = $\int (7 + 0.04q)dq$ and we want to find

$$\int_{300}^{400} (7 + 0.04q)dq = \left[7q + \frac{0.04}{2}q^2 \right]_{300}^{400}$$

$$= [7q + 0.02q^2 \,]_{300}^{400}$$

$$= (7(400) + 0.02(160,000)) - (7(300) + 0.02(90,000)) = 2,100$$

The costs will increase by £2,100.

183

Question

22

Marginal revenue $= 80 - 0.5q$

$\therefore$ Total revenue $= \int (80 - 0.5q)dq$

We wish to know the value of $\int_{12}^{16} (80 - 0.5q)dq$

$$= \left[80q - \frac{0.5}{2}q^2 \right]_{12}^{16}$$

$$= \left[80q - 0.25q^2 \right]_{12}^{16}$$

$$= ((80 \times 16) - 0.25(16^2)) - ((80 \times 12) - 0.25(12^2)) = 292$$

Total daily revenue will increase by £292.

23

The increase in profit will be equal to the increase in revenue *less* the increase in costs. We already know the increase in revenue, from question 22. We need to calculate the increase in costs:

Marginal cost $= 1 + q$

$\therefore$ Total cost $= \int (1 + q)dq$

we wish to know the value of $\int_{12}^{16} (1 + q)dq$

$$= \left[q + \frac{1q^2}{2} \right]_{12}^{16}$$

$$= \left(16 + \frac{16^2}{2} \right) - \left(12 + \frac{12^2}{2} \right) = 60$$

The total daily cost will increase by £60.

We know from question 22 that total daily revenue will increase by £292

Total daily profit will increase by £292 - £60 = £232.

Question

24   Using Economic Order Quantity $= \sqrt{\dfrac{2cd}{h}} = \sqrt{\dfrac{2 \times 5 \times 4{,}225}{0.10}} = 650$ units

25   Notice that we are given the cost of storing a unit for one *month*.

We must convert this cost to the same time period as for the demand - one *year* - by multiplying by 12.

Using Economic Order Quantity $= \sqrt{\dfrac{2cd}{h}} = \sqrt{\dfrac{2 \times 20 \times 45{,}000}{0.15 \times 12}} = 1{,}000$ units

26   In this question, stock replenishment is gradual, therefore we must use the formula:

$$EBQ = \sqrt{\dfrac{2cd}{h(1 - \dfrac{d}{r})}} = \sqrt{\dfrac{2 \times 75 \times 400}{0.10 \left(1 - \dfrac{400}{1{,}000}\right)}} = 1{,}000 \text{ units}$$

27   Total costs = stockholding costs + ordering costs $= C = \dfrac{Qh}{2} + \dfrac{cd}{Q}$

Differentiating C with respect to Q gives $\dfrac{dC}{dQ} = \dfrac{h}{2} - \dfrac{cd}{Q^2}$

At minimum total cost, this equals zero, so

$$\dfrac{h}{2} = \dfrac{cd}{Q^2}$$

Multiply both sides by Q:

$$\dfrac{Qh}{2} = \dfrac{cd}{Q}$$

Thus stockholding costs equal ordering costs at mimimum total cost, so their ratio is 1:1.

185

3: MARKING SCHEDULE

Question	Correct answer	Marks for correct answer	Question	Correct answer	Marks for correct answer	Question	Correct answer	Marks for correct answer
1	C	1	13	C	1	25	B	1
2	A	1	14	C	1	26	B	1
3	B	1	15	C	1	27	C	2
4	B	1	16	C	1	28	A	1
5	D	1	17	C	1	29	A	1
6	C	1	18	A	1	30	B	1
7	B	1	19	C	1	31	D	1
8	C	1	20	D	1	32	C	1
9	B	1	21	B	1	33	C	1
10	A	1	22	C	1	34	D	2
11	B	1	23	B	1			
12	B	2	24	B	1			

YOUR MARKS

Total marks available   37   Your total mark

GUIDELINES - If your mark was:

0 - 10   Poor. This topic is obviously causing you a great deal of difficulty. Go back to your study text and try to get to grips with it.

21 - 29   Good. Your knowledge still isn't perfect, but you are well on the way to a thorough understanding

11 - 20   Fair. Still quite a few weaknesses. You need to revise your study materials again and then attempt the questions once more.

30 - 37   Very good. You clearly understand the principles of compounding and discounting.

COMMENTS

Question

1

Using the simple interest formula $S_n = P + nrP$, the investment of £2,000 will grow to

$$S_n = £2,000 + £(8 \times 0.12 \times 2,000) = £3,920$$

This £3,920 includes both the original investment and the interest earned.

2

Using for formula for simple interest, $I_n = nrP$, the interest earned in 10 years would be

$$I_n = £(10 \times 0.144 \times 1,200) = £1,728$$

3

The interest rate is given for a month therefore we must convert 3 years to months by multiplying by 12. Using $I_n = nrP$, the interest earned in 3 years would be

$$I_n = £(3 \times 12 \times 0.02 \times 700) = £504$$

4

Interest earned in 4 years = 48 months is £1,548 - £900 = £648.
Using $I_n = nrP$,

$$648 = 48 \times r \times 900 \quad \text{where r is the monthly interest rate}$$

$$r = \frac{648}{48 \times 900} = 0.015, \text{ or } 1.5\%.$$

5

Using the compound interest formula $S_n = P(1 + r)^n$, £2,250 will in 4 years grow to

$$S_n = £2,250(1 + 0.16)^4 = £4,074$$

6

Using the compound interest formula $S_n = P(1 + r)^n$, we need to calculate the value of the investment after 6 years:

	£
$S_n = £1,350(1 + 0.12)^6$	2,665
less principal invested	1,350
= interest earned	1,315

Question

7

In the compound interest formula $S_n = P(1 + r)^n$, we know the value of S_n, r and n, and we wish to determine the value of P:

$$£23,914 = P(1 + 0.11)^{10}$$

$$\therefore \quad P = \frac{£23,914}{(1.11)^{10}} = £8,422$$

8

We know the value of P, S_n and n in the compound interest formula $S_n = P(1 + r)^n$, and we want to find the value of r:

$$£6,740 = £600(1 + r)^{15}$$

$$(1 + r)^{15} = \frac{£6,740}{£600}$$

$$1 + r = \sqrt[15]{\frac{6,740}{600}}$$

$$= 1.1750$$
$$r = 0.1750$$

The annual interest rate is 17.50%.

9

The number of years growth = 4
Let r be the annual percentage growth rate

$$(1 + r)^4 = 1.53$$
$$1 + r = (1.53)^{\frac{1}{4}}$$
$$= 1.1122$$
$$r = 0.1122$$

The annual percentage growth rate is 11.22%.

10

From the beginning of 1974 to the end of 1978 is 15 years growth.

Let r be the annual percentage growth rate, and using $S_n = P(1 + r)^n$

$$£61,482 = £2,500(1 + r)^{15}$$

$$(1 + r)^{15} = \frac{£61,482}{£2,500}$$

Continued...

Question

$$1 + r = \sqrt[15]{\frac{61,482}{2,500}}$$

$$= 1.2380$$

$$r = 0.2380$$

The annual percentage growth rate is 23.8%.

11 We must use the formula $S_n = P(1 + r)^n$, with a different number of years for each interest rate:

$$S_n = £8,000(1 + 0.08)^4 (1 + 0.12)^6 = £8,000(1.3605)(1.9738) = £21,483$$

12 The calculation must be performed in two stages:

(i) £5,000 invested for 1st 3 years = 5,000 x $(1.09)^3$ =

	£
	6,475.15
less withdrawal	1,500.00
= Balance invested for remaining 2 years	4,975.15

(ii) Value of investment after remaining 2 years = £4,975.15 x $(1.09)^2$ = £5,911

13 The price after 5 years will be £4,000 x $(1.08)^3$ $(1.10)^2$ = £4,000(1.2597)(1.21) = £6,097.

14 APR = $(1 + 0.0225)^{12} - 1$ = 30.6% per annum

15 A nominal rate of 10% per annum, payable quarterly, is an effective interest rate of $(10 \div 4)\%$ = 2.5% compound payable 4 times per year.

$$APR = (1 + 0.025)^4 - 1 = 10.4\% \text{ per annum}$$

16 The £700 invested at the beginning has earned 10% interest for 10 years, the £700 invested in Year 2 has earned 10% interest for 9 years, and so on. The last £700 invested in year 10 will have earned 10% interest for 1 year. Therefore we need to find the sum of the geometric progression:

$$£700(1.1 + 1.1^2 + 1.1^3 + ... + 1.1^{10})$$

Continued...

Question

The first term, a, is equal to (£700 x 1.1). The common ratio, r = 1.1

Using the formula $\quad S_n \quad = a \dfrac{(1 - r^n)}{(1 - r)}$

$$S_n \quad = (£700 \times 1.1) \times \dfrac{(1 - 1.1^{10})}{(1 - 1.1)} \quad = \quad £12,272$$

17 Present value $= \dfrac{£5,000}{(1.08)^6} \quad = \quad £3,151$

18 Net present value $= -£10,000 + \dfrac{£6,000}{1.1} + \dfrac{£8,000}{(1.1)^4} \quad = \quad £919$

19 The formula for discounting a future cash flow is

$$\text{Present value} \quad = \quad \dfrac{S_n}{(1 + r)^n}$$

where S_n = sum to be received
$\quad\quad r$ = rate of return
$\quad\quad n$ = number of years

Substituting the data from the question, we have

$$\text{Present value} \quad = \quad \dfrac{£18,000}{(1.14)^4}$$

20 We need to find the present value of £60,000 received in three years time. Using the same formula as for the previous question, we have

$$\text{Sum to be invested} \quad = \quad \dfrac{£60,000}{(1.12)^3}$$

21 Amount to be invested $= (£8,000 \times 0.83) + (£6,000 \times 0.62) \quad = \quad £10,360$

Question

22 Since the annual cash flow is constant, we can use the cumulative present value factors. The 8 year factor for 11% from this table is 5.15.

Present value = 5.15 x £1,400 = £7,210

23 Again using the table of cumulative present value factors, we require the 15% factor for years 3 to 7. We can get this by taking the factor for years 1-7 which is just the total of the individual factors for years 1, 2....7, and subtracting the factor for years 1-2.

Present value of £1 per annum for years 1-7 at 15%	= 4.16
less present value of £1 per annum for years 1-2 at 15%	1.63
= present value of £1 per annum for years 3 - 7 at 15%	2.53
x annual cash flow	£1,800
= present value of cash flow	£4,554

24 From the cumulative present value factors table:

£

		£
Present value of £1 per annum for years 1-8 at 13%	= 4.80	
less present value of £1 per annum for years 1-3 at 13%	= 2.36	
= present value of £1 per annum for years 4-8 at 13%	2.44	
x annual cash flow, years 4-8	£2,200	
= present value of cash flows in years 4-8		5,368
Present value of cash flows in years 1-3 = £2,000 x 2.36 =		4,720
Present value of cash flows, years 1-8		10,088
less initial cost of project		3,400
Net present value of project		6,688

25

Year	Cash flow	Discount factor at 16%	Present value
	£		£
0	(5,000)	1.00	(5,000)
1	(2,000)	0.86	(1,720)
2	7,000	0.74	5,180
3	6,000	0.64	3,840
Net present value			2,300

26 The amount to be repaid each year $= \dfrac{£12,000}{\text{PV factor of £1 per annum at 14\% for 8 years}}$

$$= \frac{£12,000}{4.64}$$

$$= £2,586$$

Question

27 The first thing that we need to calculate is the PV factor of £1 per annum at 11% for years 6 to 10:

From cumulative present value tables:

present value of £1 per annum for years 1-10 at 11%	= 5.89
less present value of £1 per annum for years 1-5 at 11%	= 3.70
= present value of £1 per annum for years 6-10 at 11%	2.19

Let the annual repayment in years 6-10 be A

$$£40,000 = \text{present value of repayments} + \text{present value of repayments}$$
$$\text{in years 1-5} \qquad\qquad \text{in years 6-10}$$

$$= [£5,000 \times 3.70] + [A \times 2.19]$$
$$2.19 \, A = £40,000 - £18,500$$
$$= £21,500$$
$$\therefore \quad A = £9,817 \text{ (to the nearest £)}$$

The annual repayment in years 6 to 10 will be £9,817.

28
$$\text{Amount repaid each year} = \frac{\text{Amount of the loan}}{\text{Annuity factor at 13\% per annum for 6 years}}$$

$$\therefore \text{amount of the loan} = £12,000 \times 4.00$$
$$= £48,000$$

29 The present value of a perpetuity is $\dfrac{a}{r}$

where r is the discount rate.

	£
Present value of cash inflows $= \dfrac{£2,100}{0.14} =$	15,000
less initial investment	13,000
Net present value of project	2,000

30 The six year annuity factor must be £3,000/£709 = 4.23. This is found under 11% for in years 1-6 in annuity tables.

31 Since £804 is received immediately, one is effectively investing £(5,000 - 804) = £4,196 now to secure an annuity of £804 for ten years, starting one year from now. The ten year annuity factor must be £4,196/£804 = 5.22. This is found in tables under 14% for years 1-10.

Question

32

The perpetuity factor is $\frac{1}{r}$, so

$$\frac{1}{r} = \frac{3,750}{514}$$

$$r = \frac{514}{3,750} = 0.1371 = 13.71\%.$$

33

$$IRR \simeq 10 + \frac{4,000}{4,000 - -2,000} (15 - 10) = 13.33\%$$

34

Time	Cash flow	10% Discount factor	PV	20% Disccount factor	PV
	£		£		£
0	(10,000)	1	(10,000)	1	(10,000)
1	6,000	0.91	5,460	0.83	4,980
3	8,000	0.75	6,000	0.58	4,640
			1,460		(380)

$$IRR \simeq 10 + \frac{1,460}{1,460 - -380} (20 - 10) = 10 + \frac{1,460}{1,840} \times 10 = 17.93\% \simeq 18\%.$$

4: MARKING SCHEDULE

Question	Correct answer	Marks for the correct answer	Question	Correct answer	Marks for the correct answer
1	A	1	13	C	1
2	C	1	14	C	1
3	C	1	15	C	1
4	D	1	16	B	1
5	C	1	17	A	1
6	B	1	18	A	1
7	B	1	19	D	2
8	C	1	20	B	2
9	C	1	21	B	1
10	B	1	22	B	1
11	C	1	23	D	2
12	B	1			

YOUR MARKS

Total marks available   26   Your total mark

GUIDELINES - If your mark was:

0 - 8
Poor. The important techniques in this chapter are causing you difficulty. Go back to your study text and work through each relevant section carefully, before trying this chapter again.

9 - 13
Fair. Several of the questions have caught you out. If there are one or two particular techniques which have caused you problems go back to your study text and read through the relevant sections carefully.

14 - 21
Good. There may be a particular group of questions which has caused you difficulty. Check whether this is so, and refer to your study text if there is a clear gap in your knowledge.

22 - 26
Very good. You have a thorough understanding of the principles of depreciation and discounts.

COMMENTS

Question

1

The annual charge for depreciation will be $\dfrac{£(16,000 - 1,000)}{8}$ = £1,875

2

The lease is being amortised over 20 years in total. The original purchase price is therefore 20 x £3,700 = £74,000.

3

The annual charge for amortisation should be $\dfrac{£(36,000 - 6,000)}{10}$ = £3,000

4

Annual depreciation of the delivery vehicle = $\dfrac{£(15,000 - 1,000)}{4}$ = £3,500

∴ the net book value after 3 years
    = original purchase price *less* depreciation to date
    = £15,000 - (3 x £3,500)
    = £4,500

5

The sum of the digits is 20 + 19 + 18 + ... + 1 (an arithmetic progression)

Using $S_n = \dfrac{n}{2}(a+z)$, the sum $= \dfrac{20}{2}(1+20)$

                         = 210.

The total amount to be depreciated is £(73,500 - 10,500) =   £63,000
∴ The depreciation cost per digit = £63,000 ÷ 210   =   £300

Depreciation in the first year = 20 digits   = 20 x £300
                             = £6,000

6

The digits assigned to year 1 = 20 digits
                 to year 2 = 19 digits (20-1)
                 to year 3 = 18 digits (20-2)

∴ digits assigned to year 12   = (20-11) = 9 digits
∴ depreciation in twelfth year   = 9 x £300 = £2,700

Question

7

	£	£
Original cost of the asset		73,500
less depreciation - year 1 300 x 20	6,000	
- year 2 300 x 19	5,700	
- year 3 300 x 18	5,400	17,100
Net book value after 3 years		56,400

8

The workings for this question and the next four questions set out the depreciation charge year by year. The workings for later questions on reducing balance depreciation use formulae. Both approaches give the same answers.

	£
Cost	14,000
Depreciation year 1	(2,800)
	11,200
Depreciation year 2	(2,240)
	8,960
Depreciation year 3	(1,792)
	7,168

9

	£	Cumulative depreciation £
Cost	22,000	
Depreciation year 1	(5,500)	5,500
	16,500	
Depreciation year 2	(4,125)	4,125
	12,375	
Depreciation year 3	(3,094)	3,094
	9,281	
Depreciation year 4	(2,320)	2,320
	6,961	
Total depreciation years 1 - 4		15,039

10 - 12

	£	Cumulative depreciation £
Cost	18,000	
Depreciation year 1	(2,700)	2,700
	15,300	
Depreciation year 2	(2,295)	2,295
	13,005	
Depreciation year 3	(1,951)	1,951
	11,054	
Depreciation year 4	(1,658)	1,658
	9,396	
Depreciation year 5	(1,409)	1,409
c/f	7,897	
Total depreciation years 1-5 (question 11)		10,013

Continued...

Question

	£
b/f	7,897
Depreciation year 6 (question 10)	(1,198)
	6,789
Depreciation year 7	(1,018)
	5,771
Depreciation year 8	(866)
Net book value after 8 years (question 12)	4,905

13 The net book value of an asset at the end of year n is given by $A(1-r)^n$, where r is the reducing balance depreciation rate as a proportion. Since the net book value at the end of year 6 needs to be £1,500,

$$£1,500 = £25,000(1-r)^6$$
$$\therefore \quad (1-r)^6 = \frac{£1,500}{£25,000}$$
$$= 0.06$$
$$1-r = \sqrt[6]{0.06}$$
$$= 0.63$$
$$\therefore \quad r = 0.37$$

The annual rate of depreciation is 37%.

14 Using the formula for the net book value of an asset, $A(1-r)^n$, the residual value R is given by

$$R = £34,000 (1 - 0.18)^8$$
$$= £34,000 \times 0.2044$$
$$= £6,950$$

15 Using the formula for the net book value of an asset, $A(1-r)^n$, we know that the net book value of the furniture at the end of year 6 will be £1,000:

$$£1,000 = £10,000(1-r)^6$$
$$(1-r)^6 = \frac{£1,000}{£10,000}$$
$$= 0.10$$
$$1-r = \sqrt[6]{0.10}$$
$$= 0.68$$
$$r = 0.32$$

The annual rate of depreciation is 32%.

Question

16

We want to find the third term in the geometric progression.

$$
\begin{aligned}
\text{Using nth term} &= ar^{n-1}\\
\text{first term, a} &= \text{£10,000} \times 0.32 \text{ (the depreciation rate from question 15)}\\
r &= (1 - 0.32) = 0.68\\
\therefore \quad \text{3rd term} &= \text{£10,000} \times 0.32 \times (0.68)^2\\
&= \text{£1,480}
\end{aligned}
$$

The depreciation charge in the third year will be £1,480.

17

Using the formula for the net book value of an asset, $A(1-r)^n$, and the depreciation rate of 32% calculated in question 15:

$$
\begin{aligned}
\text{net book value after five years} &= \text{£10,000} (1 - 0.32)^5\\
&= \text{£1,454}
\end{aligned}
$$

18

The money invested at the end of the first year will earn 15% interest for four years; the investment at the end of the second year will earn 15% interest for three years and so on. The sum of the amounts invested and all interest earned must be equal to £24,000. If £A is the amount invested each year, the total value of the fund after five years will be

$$A + A(1 + 0.15) + A(1 + 0.15)^2 + A(1 + 0.15)^3 + A(1 + 0.15)^4$$

This is a geometric progression with first term A, and common ratio 1.15, so we can use the geometric progression formula.

$$S_n = \frac{a(1-r^n)}{(1-r)}$$

$$24,000 = A\frac{(1 - 1.15^5)}{(1 - 1.15)}$$

$$\therefore \quad A = \frac{24,000(1 - 1.15)}{(1 - 1.15^5)}$$

$$= 3,560$$

The amount to be invested at the end of each year is £3,560

Question

19

Annual interest of 10% per annum compounded every six months for two years is equivalent to 5% interest credited for four time periods. Once again we can use the formula for a geometric progression:

$$S_n = \frac{a(1 - r^n)}{(1 - r)}$$

$$17{,}000 = a\frac{(1 - 1.05^4)}{(1 - 1.05)}$$

$$a = \frac{17{,}000(1 - 1.05)}{(1 - 1.05^4)}$$
$$= 3{,}944$$

The amount to be invested at the end of each six month period is £3,944.

20

This question is similar to question 18, except that the investments are to be made at the beginning of each year. If £A is invested each year, the total value of the fund after three years will be $A(1 + 0.12) + A(1 + 0.12)^2 + A(1 + 0.12)^3$. The first term of this geometric progression is 1.12A, and the common ratio is 1.12.

$$\text{Using } S_n = a\frac{(1 - r^n)}{(1 - r)}$$

$$5{,}000 = 1.12A\frac{(1 - 1.12^3)}{(1 - 1.12)}$$

$$1.12A = \frac{5{,}000(1 - 1.12)}{(1 - 1.12^3)}$$
$$= 1{,}482$$
$$A = 1{,}323$$

The amount to be invested each year is £1,323.

21

The discount is £(2,500 - 2,000) = £500.

As a percentage of the invoice price, this is $\frac{£500}{£2{,}500} \times 100\% = 20\%$

Question

22

	£
Invoice value of goods before discount	18,000
less 5% trade discount	900
	17,100
less 6% settlement discount	1,026
Cash actually received	16,074

23

		£
Half of the customers will deduct a 2% settlement discount:		
∴ amount received - £35,400 x 0.5 x 0.98	=	17,346
One fifth (20%) of customers will deduct 10% trade discount:		
∴ amount received = £35,400 x 0.2 x 0.9	=	6,372
The remaining 30% of customers will not deduct any discount:		
∴ amount received = £35,400 x 0.3	=	10,620
Cash received from July sales		34,338

5: MARKING SCHEDULE

Question	Correct answer	Marks for correct answer	Question	Correct answer	Marks for correct answer	Question	Correct answer	Marks for correct answer
1	C	1	15	B	1	29	C	1
2	A	1	16	A	1	30	B	1
3	C	1	17	D	1	31	C	1
4	B	1	18	C	1	32	B	1
5	D	1	19	D	1	33	C	1
6	B	1	20	C	1	34	B	1
7	D	1	21	C	1	35	A	1
8	C	1	22	B	1	36	C	1
9	D	1	23	C	1	37	C	1
10	D	1	24	C	1	38	A	1
11	B	1	25	D	1	39	B	1
12	B	1	26	C	1	40	C	1
13	A	1	27	D	2			
14	D	1	28	A	1			

YOUR MARKS

Total marks available   **41**   Your total mark

GUIDELINES - If your mark was:

| 0 - 12 | Poor. This topic is causing you great difficulty. Go back to your study text and concentrate particularly on the graphical presentation of data. |

| 13 - 21 | Fair. You are still weak in this important area of business mathematics. Think carefully about the reasons for your errors. |

| 22 - 33 | Good. Although you still have to perfect your knowledge, you are well on the way to a thorough understanding. |

| 34 - 41 | Very good. You have a thorough understanding of the collection and presentation of statistical data. |

COMMENTS

Question

1

The Monthly Digest of Statistics and Economic Trends are both secondary data provided by the government. Historic sales data were not collected specifically for the preparation of forecasts, therefore they are also secondary data. Data collected through personal interview for a particular project are primary data.

3

An *attribute* is a property which cannot be quantified - for example there is no degree of 'maleness', or of 'singleness'. On the other hand, height and weight can be quantified and are known as *variables*.

4

A discrete variable is one which can only take on one of a specified set of values, therefore variables 1 and 2 are discrete. Variable 3 can take on any value and is therefore a continuous variable.

5

The method described is systematic sampling, whereby every fourth item is selected after a random start.

6

Since every fourth item is selected, the sampling interval is 4.

7

It is a stratified sample because the population is split up into strata (layers).

8

The total number of employees is 1,000. A sample of 200 is therefore a 20% sample. Those employed for up to 3 years will be in the first two strata:

Length of service	Number of employees		Number in sample
up to 1 year	100	x 20%	20
more than 1 year, up to 3 years	365	x 20%	<u>73</u>
Number in sample who have been employed for up to 3 years			<u><u>93</u></u>

Question

9   The sample is selected in stages, at first selecting not individuals but constituencies.

10   The total sample size will be 50 x 5 x 30 = 7,500 people.

11   This is quota sampling because the interviewers merely have to find enough people of each description.

12   Since there is a 6 in the third decimal place, we round up to 726.59.

13   The zero counts as a significant figure, therefore 2, 9 and 0 are the first three significant figures. Since the fourth figure is a 3, we do not round up to 29.1

14   We want five digits, and there are three before the decimal point, so we round to two decimal places.

15   If each of the production volumes has been rounded to the nearest thousand units, the maximum error in each individual figure is ± 500 units.

∴ the maximum error for three factories   = 3 x 500
                                              = ± 1,500 units
The true production volume therefore lies in the range 31,000 ± 1,500 units
                                      or 29,500 to 32,500 units

16   If each of the production volumes has been rounded up to the nearest thousand units, the maximum error in each individual figure is 999 units. Therefore the maximum error for three factories is 2,997 units. As the figures have been rounded up, the true total production volume could be 2,997 units lower, and therefore lies in the range 28,003 to 31,000 units.

Question

17 As for question 16, the maximum error for three factories is 2,997 units. However, as the figures have been rounded down, the true total production volume could be 2,997 units higher, and therefore lies in the range 31,000 to 33,997 units.

18 The maximum error in each figure is ± £500, therefore the average error for each figure is one half of £500, ie £250.

Rounding to the nearest thousand is an unbiased approximation, as errors could go in either direction and will cancel each other out to some extent, therefore the average error in 9 values is $\sqrt{9}$ x £250 = 3 x £250 = ± £750. This shows us the total error we can reasonably expect, and we should then consider whether such an error would be acceptable.

19 The maximum error in any figure due to rounding up to the nearest thousand is + £1,000. The average error for each individual figure is one half this amount, ie £500.

Rounding up is a biased approximation, as all rounding is in the same direction and errors cannot cancel each other out. The average error is 9 x £500 = £4,500.

20 If each sales figure has been rounded to the nearest ten units, the maximum error in each individual figure is ± 5 units.

∴ The maximum error in 16 periods $= 16 \times 5$
$$= \pm\ 80\ \text{units.}$$

21 For unbiased approximations, the average error in total is equal to $\sqrt{n}$ x the average error in individual figures.

Average error per period = half of the maximum error per period
$$= \pm\ 0.5 \times 5 = \pm\ 2.5\ \text{units}$$

Average error $= \sqrt{16} \times 2.5$
$$= \pm\ 10\ \text{units}$$

22 The maximum relative error is:

$$\frac{80\ \text{units}}{8,820\ \text{units}} \times 100\% = 0.9\%$$

This shows that any error will be small relative to the size of the data, so will probably not be very serious.

Question

23 The maximum error in each estimate is ± £5,000. When one rounded number is subtracted from another rounded number, the maximum error is the sum of the individual errors, ie 2 x £5,000 = ± £10,000.

24 First calculate the highest possible total expenditure:

		£	£
Doughnuts - maximum number purchased = 450 + 8% = 486 x } x maximum price = 0.10 + 10% = 0.11 }			53.46
Cream buns - maximum number purchased = 275 + 8% = 297 x } x maximum price = 0.20 + 10% = 0.22 }			65.34
Maximum total expenditure			118.80

Expected expenditure:

Doughnuts = 450 x 0.10	45.00	
Cream buns = 275 x 0.20	55.00	100.00
Maximum absolute error		£18.80

$$\therefore \text{Maximum relative error in forecast total expenditure} = \pm \frac{£18.80}{£100.00} \times 100\%$$

$$= \pm 18.8\%$$

25 Calculate the maximum absolute error, and then convert this to the maximum relative error. Remember that, even if figures are subtracted from each other, the maximum error is the sum of the individual errors.

	Forecast	Relative error	Maximum absolute error
	£'000		£'000
Sales revenue	760	± 1%	± 7.6
Labour costs	240	± 5%	± 12.0
Material costs	280	± 6%	± 16.8
Other costs	180	± 3%	± 5.4
			± 41.8

The forecast profit, in £'000, is 760 - (240 + 280 + 180) = 60

$$\therefore \text{The maximum relative error in the profit forecast} = \pm \frac{41.8}{60.0} \times 100\%$$

$$= \pm 70\%$$

This shows that a very large error, relative to the size of the forecast profit, is possible, so the forecast may not be worth much.

Question

26

The machines which definitely dispensed less than 20g in total are all those in the top row, all those in the left hand column, and the 72 machines which dispensed at least 5g but under 10g of each product. The machines which dispensed 5g - under 10g of one product and 10g - under 15g of the other might have dispensed under 20g in total, but could have dispensed more (for example, 9g of one product and 14g of the other, totalling 23g). The required number of machines is therefore 37 + 46 + 28 + 45 + 12 + 72 = 240

27

We must fill in missing figures one by one. Each new figure enables us to work out another one.

Total sales for all shops for week 1 are 96,500 - (25,400 + 28,000 + 25,500) = £17,600.
Sales for shop Q for week 1 are 17,600 - (5,000 + 3,000 + 2,700 + 1,900) = £5,000.
Sales for shop S for week 2 are 20,000 - (2,700 + 6,000 + 5,000) = £6,300.
Sales for shop Q for week 2 are 25,400 - (7,200 + 4,000 + 6,300 + 2,000) = £5,900.
Sales for shop R for week 4 are 16,000 - (3,000 + 4,000 + 5,000) = £4,000.
Sales for shop Q for week 4 are 25,500 - (6,900 + 4,000 + 5,000 + 2,100) = £7,500
Total sales for shop Q are 5,000 + 5,900 + 8,000 + 7,500 = £26,400

28

Frequencies of calls and geographical areas should not both appear in the rows, nor both in the columns, as in C. B does not accommodate people who make precisely 5 calls a day, nor does D accommodate those who make precisely 10 calls a day. A covers all possible numbers of calls.

29

Nine students scored at least 60 marks, but less than 80 marks. Three students scored at least 80 marks. The number scoring 60 marks or more is therefore 9 + 3 = 12, out of a total of 34 students.

$\therefore$ percentage scoring 60 marks or more = $\dfrac{12}{34}$ x 100% = 35.3%.

30

The total production cost is equal to £(8,325 + 6,475 + 3,700) = £18,500.
The total number of degrees in the circle is 360, and we need to know the number of degrees per £1 of cost:

$$\frac{360^0}{£18,500} = 0.01946^0 \text{ per £1 of cost}$$

Therefore, x^0, representing direct materials = 8,325 x 0.01946^0
= 162^0

Do keep clear the difference between ^{0} for degrees of angle, as here, and ^{0} as an index, giving a number to the power 0 (see chapter 1). The two have nothing to do with each other.

Question

31 Using the data in question 30, y^0, representing direct labour $= 6,475 \times 0.01946^0$
$= 126^0$

32 The Venn diagram, with all the numbers entered, is as follows:

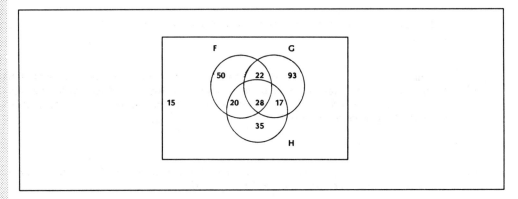

$22 = 120 - (50 + 20 + 28)$ people like F and G but not H

$160 - (22 + 28) = 110$ people like G but not F

$100 - (20 + 28) = 52$ people like H but not F.

$280 - (120 + 15) = 145$ people like G or H or both but not F

Since $110 + 52 = 162$, $162 - 145 = 17$ people must like G and H but not F, so

$110 - 17 = 93$ people like G only, and

$52 - 17 = 35$ people like H only

33 If a bar for 2,120 employees (the 19X5 total) was 10.6 cm high, the scale must be

$$\frac{10.6}{2,120} = 0.005 \text{ cm per employee.}$$

A segment for 1,450 employees (19X6, grade 4) will therefore have a height of

$1,450 \times 0.005 = 7.25$ cm

Question

34

We must first determine what percentage of total sales revenue was attributable to division W, as follows:

Division	Ratio of sales	Percentage of sales
V	3 x 2 = 6	6 x 100/9 = 66.7
W	2 x 1 = 2	2 x 100/9 = 22.2
X	1	1 x 100/9 = 11.1
	9	100.0

The height of the segment representing W's sales is therefore 15 cm x 22.2% = 3.33 cm.

35

In a histogram the frequencies of the data are represented by the *areas* of the bars. If we choose a standard class interval of four hours, we then need to divide the frequency of the first group by three, and the frequency of the last group by two. The graph for these adjusted frequencies is graph 1.

36

In this example, a standard class interval of £40 can be used. The frequencies for the last two intervals therefore need to be adjusted:

Class interval	Size of interval	Frequency	Adjustment	Adjusted frequency
£	£			
> 160 ≤ 180	20	6	x 40/20	12
> 180 ≤ 240	60	3	x 40/60	2

The adjusted frequencies indicate the correct heights of the bars in the histogram, therefore graph 3 is correct. Graph 2 has the correct heights for the bars, but the intervals on the horizontal axis are not drawn correctly.

37

Statement 1 is correct, because the ogive shows cumulative frequencies. Statement 2 is correct, because the graph exceeds 600 on the cumulative frequency axis. Statement 3 is incorrect, because the ogive tells us that a cumulative total of 200 employees produced less than 1,000 units. Some of those 2,000 will have produced, for example, only 500 units.

38

The ogive shows the number of times that weekly output *exceeded* a certain value. For example, we can see that output exceeded zero on all 80 occasions, but that weekly output never exceeded 500 units. Therefore, the data pair marked shows that output *exceeded* 200 units on 50 occasions, therefore Statements 2 and 3 are both incorrect. Statement 1 is correct.

Question

39

The three pieces of information which the manager requires can be obtained from the three lines on a Z chart - the moving annual total will give a comparison of the current levels of performance with those of the previous year.

40

Statement 1 is incorrect. If it were true, then the curve would be near to the diagonal line of no concentration, because a large percentage of customers would correspond to a large percentage of sales.

Statement 2 is correct for both years, and Statement 3 is correct because the year 2 line is closer to the diagonal line of no concentration than the year 1 line.

6: MARKING SCHEDULE

Question	Correct answer	Marks for correct answer	Question	Correct answer	Marks for correct answer	Question	Correct answer	Marks for correct answer
1	B	1	20	C	1	39	C	2
2	B	1	21	C	1	40	D	2
3	C	1	22	B	1	41	B	1
4	C	1	23	C	1	42	A	1
5	D	1	24	D	2	43	C	1
6	B	1	25	A	1	44	D	1
7	C	1	26	D	1	45	C	1
8	A	1	27	C	2	46	B	1
9	C	1	28	C	2	47	C	1
10	B	1	29	D	2	48	D	1
11	D	1	30	D	1	49	C	1
12	A	1	31	C	2	50	B	1
13	A	1	32	D	1	51	B	1
14	C	2	33	D	1	52	D	1
15	C	1	34	A	1	53	B	1
16	B	1	35	B	1	54	B	1
17	B	1	36	B	1	55	C	1
18	A	1	37	A	1	56	B	1
19	B	1	38	D	2	57	B	1

YOUR MARKS

Total marks available   66   Your total mark

6: MARKING SCHEDULE

GUIDELINES - If your mark was:

0 - 20
You need to revise the concepts of probability thoroughly. Go back to your study text and work through the relevant chapters again.

34 - 52
Good. Although there are still some gaps in your knowledge, you are well on the way to a thorough understanding of probability.

21 - 33
You are still not quite fluent with probability calculations. Read the comments carefully and make sure that you understand the reasons for your errors.

53 - 66
Very good. You have a broad and thorough understanding of the principles of probability.

COMMENTS

Question

1

The data tell us that there was a machine breakdown on 120 days out of a total of 480. The probability of a breakdown is therefore:

$$\frac{120}{480} \times 100\% = 25\%$$

2

A demand of 53 units has occurred on 42 days out of a total of 200. Expressed as a percentage, the probability is $\frac{42}{200} \times 100\% = 21\%$.

3

Factory	Ratio of visits
North	1
South	2
West	1
	4

∴ Probability of visiting the North factory = $\frac{1}{4}$ = 0.25

4

Total units scrapped in all 4 processes	= 420 + 208 + 125 + 87 = 840
Completed units from an input of 4,000	= 4,000 - 840 = 3,160
Probability of unit being completed	= $\frac{3,160}{4,000} \times 100\%$
	= 79.0%

5

Units scrapped in processes 1 and 2	= 420 + 208 = 628
Units entering process 3	= 4,000 - 628 = 3,372
Probability of a unit entering process 3	= $\frac{3,372}{4,000} \times 100\%$
	= 84.3%

Question

6

Of 4,000 units entering the production line, 420 will be scrapped in process 1 and 208 in process 2. This leaves 4,000 - (420 + 208) = 3,372 which make it as far as process 3. Of these, 125 will be scrapped in process 3.

The required probability is therefore $\dfrac{125}{3,372} = 0.037$

7

Since probabilities must total 100%, the probability of the pessimistic outcome occurring is 10%.

Outcome	Profit/(Loss) £	Probability	Expected value £
Optimistic	19,200	30%	5,760
Most likely	12,500	60%	7,500
Pessimistic	(6,700)	10%	(670)
		100%	
Expected value of profit			12,590

8

First, calculate the expected values of sales demand and of unit variable costs:

Sales demand (units)	Probability	Expected demand (units)
4,000	0.2	800
6,500	0.7	4,550
3,000	0.1	300
Expected value of demand		5,650

Variable cost per unit (£)	Probability	Expected value £
8.50	0.4	3.40
9.00	0.6	5.40
Expected value of variable cost per unit		8.80

We can now calculate the expected value of profit:

		£
Sales revenue	£14 x 5,650 units	79,100
Variable cost	£8.80 x 5,650 units	49,720
Contribution		29,380
Fixed cost		9,400
Expected value of profit		19,980

9

There are $_9C_3$ ways of selecting three out of nine people:

$$_9C_3 = \frac{9!}{6!\,3!} = \frac{9 \times 8 \times 7}{3 \times 2} = 84 \text{ ways}$$

213

Question

10   There are $_8C_2$ ways of selecting two out of eight candidates:

$$_8C_2 = \frac{8!}{6!\,2!} = \frac{8 \times 7}{2} = 28 \text{ ways}$$

11   If the order of the selection is significant, we have to calculate the number of permutations of two candidates from eight:

$$_8P_2 = \frac{8!}{6!} = 8 \times 7 = 56 \text{ ways}$$

12   There are $_7C_4$ ways of selecting four out of seven projects:

$$_7C_4 = \frac{7!}{3!\,4!} = \frac{7 \times 6 \times 5}{3 \times 2} = 35 \text{ ways}$$

13   If the board is already committed to selecting one of the projects, the choice is now reduced to selecting three out of the remaining six available.

$$_6C_3 = \frac{6!}{3!\,3!} = \frac{6 \times 5 \times 4}{3 \times 2} = 20 \text{ ways.}$$

14   If the board must select *at least* two medium risk projects, the choices are:

(i)   to select 2 out of the 3 medium risk projects, and then 2 out of the 4 high risk projects.

medium risk: $_3C_2 = \frac{3!}{2!\,1!} = 3$

high risk: $_4C_2 = \frac{4!}{2!\,2!} = 6$

Number of combinations possible = 6 x 3 = 18

(ii)   to select all 3 medium risk projects, then 1 out of the 4 high risk projects.

Number of combinations possible = 4

Therefore, taking account of both sets of choices, the total number of combinations possible = 18 + 4 = 22.

Question

15 Since the order of the digits is significant, we have to calculate the number of the available permutations. There are 10 available digits, and we need 3 of them for each account number, so we need $_{10}P_3$.

$$_{10}P_3 = \frac{10!}{7!} = 10 \times 9 \times 8 = 720$$

16 If we are restricted to using 4 as the first digit, we need to calculate the number of permutations of the nine other digits (0 to 3 and 5 to 9) for the remaining 2 digits of the 3-digit number.

$$_9P_2 = \frac{9!}{7!} = 9 \times 8 = 72 \text{ numbers.}$$

17 The possible outcomes are mutually exclusive, as any one delivery time can only fall into one of the five classes. We can therefore just add probabilities.

P(more than 3 weeks) = P(>3 weeks ≤ 4 weeks) + P (>4 weeks ≤ 5 weeks)
= 0.25 + 0.15
= 0.40

18 Demand on any one day is independent of demand on preceding or subsequent days, so we can simply multiply probabilities.

P(15 and 15) = P(15) x P(15)
= 0.3 x 0.3
= 0.09

19 Multiplying probabilities, as in the preceding question:

P(14, 14 and 16) = P(14) x P(14) x P(16)
= 0.5 x 0.5 x 0.2
= 0.05

Question

20 Both the sales of G and the sales of H could reach £300 in the same month, so the two outcomes are not mutually exclusive. The probability that *either* of these two outcomes will occur is the sum of their probabilities *less*, to avoid double counting, the probability of both outcomes happening together:

$$P(G \text{ or } H = 300) = P(G = 300) + P(H = 300) - P(G \text{ and } H = 300)$$
$$= 0.50 + 0.30 - (0.5 \times 0.3)$$
$$= 0.65$$

21 The probability of exceeding the overdraft limit depends on whether extended credit is negotiated. If Q represents exceeding the overdraft limit and R is the *failure* to negotiate extended credit (P(R) = 0.75), then:

$$P(Q) = P(R) \times P(Q|R)$$
$$= 0.75 \times 0.60$$
$$= 0.45$$

22 We can use ratios to calculate the probability of a container being selected from machine L:

Machine	Ratio of inspection		Probability of selection
L		1	*0.10
M	(1x3)	3	0.30
N	(3x2)	6	0.60
		10	1.00

*Probability of selecting from machine L = $\dfrac{1}{10}$ = 0.10.

23 The probability of a selected container being defective can be calculated by multiplying, for each machine, the probability of selection and the probability of being defective (since the two are independent), then adding the results (since a container from one machine cannot also be from another, so these possibilities - machine L, machine M, machine N - are mutually exclusive).

Machine	Probability of selection		Probability of being defective		Probability of defective container being selected
L	0.10	x	0.10	=	0.01
M	0.30	x	0.20	=	0.06
N	0.60	x	0.25	=	0.15
Total probability					0.22

Question

24

Of all the defective containers selected, a certain proportion come from machine N. Although 60% of all containers selected come from machine N, this is not the proportion we need, because machine N has a higher proportion of defective output than the other machines. The probability that a container found to be defective comes from machine N

$$= \frac{\text{probability of defective from N}}{\text{probability of defective from L, M, N}}$$

$$= \frac{0.15}{0.22}$$

$$= 0.68$$

**25
–
26**

	Rain	No rain	Total
Played	45	440	485
Cancelled	405	110	515
Total	450	550	1,000

The bottom row is completed first:

0.45 x 1,000	= 450
1,000 - 450	= 550

The 'Cancelled' row can then be filled in:

0.9 x 450	= 405
0.2 x 550	= 110
405 + 110	= 515

The 'Played' row can then be filled in:

450 - 405	= 45
550 - 110	= 440
45 + 440	= 485

Continued...

Question

The probability of it having rained if the match was cancelled is:

Days on which match cancelled and it rained
    Days on which match cancelled

$$= \frac{405}{515} = 0.79$$

The probability of it not having rained if the match was played is:

Days on which match played and it did not rain
    Days on which match played

$$= \frac{440}{485} = 0.91$$

27

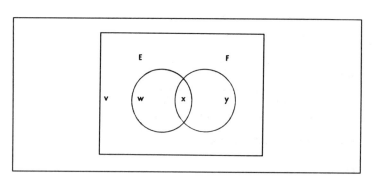

Since v, w, x and y represent all possible events:

	$v + w + x + y$	$= 1.0$	(1)
$P(\bar{E}\ or\ \bar{F})\ =$	$v + w\ \ \ \ \ + y$	$= 0.7$	(2)
$P(\bar{E}\ and\ \bar{F})\ =$	v	$= 0.2$	(3)
$P(F)\ =$	$x + y$	$= 0.4$	(4)

Substitute for (x + y) from (4) into (1):

$$v + w + 0.4 = 1.0$$
$$v + w = 0.6 \quad (5)$$

Substitute in (2) $0.6 + y = 0.7$

$$y = 0.1$$

Substitute in (4) $x = 0.3$

Substitute for v from (3) into (5):

$$0.2 + w = 0.6$$
$$w = 0.4$$
$$P(E) = w + x = 0.4 + 0.3 = 0.7$$

Question

28 We have to find $P(X|\bar{Y})$, which is the probability of X, given 'not Y'.

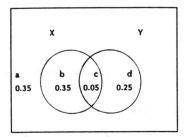

The values of a, b, c and d have been deduced as follows:

$$P(X) \ = \ b + c \ = 0.40 \ (1)$$
$$P(Y) \ = \ c + d \ = 0.30 \ (2)$$
$$P(X \text{ and } Y) \ = \ c \ = 0.05$$
$$\therefore \quad \text{in (1)} \quad b \ = 0.40 - 0.05 = 0.35$$
$$\text{in (2)} \quad d \ = 0.30 - 0.05 = 0.25$$
$$\text{and since } a + b + c + d \ = 1.0$$
$$a \ = 1.0 - 0.35 - 0.05 - 0.25$$
$$= 0.35$$
$$P(\bar{Y}) \ = \ a + b \ = 0.70$$
$$\therefore \quad P(X|\bar{Y}) \ = \ \frac{b}{a + b} \ = \frac{0.35}{0.70} \ = \ 0.50$$

29

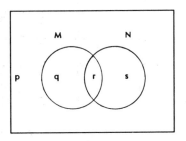

$$P(M) \quad = \ q + r \ = \ 0.50$$
$$P(M \text{ and } N) \ = \ r \quad = \ 0.15$$
$$P(\bar{M} \text{ and } \bar{N}) \ = \ p \quad = \ 0.10$$

Question

Since p + (q + r) + s   = 1.00
     0.10 + 0.50 + s   = 1.00
        s   = 1.00 - 0.10 - 0.60 = 0.40
  P(N) =   r + s   =   0.15 + 0.40
                   = 0.55

30 Either or both of the cyclists might use Everglow batteries, so the outcomes are not mutually exclusive.

Probability that at least one uses Everglow

= P(one uses Everglow) + P(the other uses Everglow) - P (both use Everglow)

$$= \frac{1}{3} + \frac{1}{3} - (\frac{1}{3} \times \frac{1}{3})$$

$$= \frac{3}{9} + \frac{3}{9} - \frac{1}{9}$$

$$= \frac{5}{9}$$

31 Probability that exactly one uses Everglow = $2 \times \frac{1}{3} \times \frac{2}{3} = \frac{4}{9}$

It may be easier for you to understand these workings if you look at the following table:

	Uses Everglow?		Probability	
	1	2		
	Y	Y	$\frac{1}{3} \times \frac{1}{3} = \frac{1}{9}$	
(Y = Yes; N = No)	Y	N	$\frac{1}{3} \times \frac{2}{3} = \frac{2}{9}$	*
	N	Y	$\frac{2}{3} \times \frac{1}{3} = \frac{2}{9}$	*
	N	N	$\frac{2}{3} \times \frac{2}{3} = \frac{4}{9}$	

The table shows all possible combinations of Everglow usage, and the probabilities therefore total 1.0. The two probabilities which must be summed to give the correct answer are marked with asterisks.

The answer to question 30 could have been obtained by adding the probabilities of YY, YN and NY:

$$\frac{1}{9} + \frac{2}{9} + \frac{2}{9} = \frac{5}{9}$$

Question

32
.
35

You could construct a table to answer these questions:

Can go 30 miles?

	V	W	Probability			
	Y	Y	$\frac{7}{8}$	$\times \frac{2}{3}$	=	$\frac{14}{24}$
(Y = Yes; N = No)	Y	N	$\frac{7}{8}$	$\times \frac{1}{3}$	=	$\frac{7}{24}$
	N	Y	$\frac{1}{8}$	$\times \frac{2}{3}$	=	$\frac{2}{24}$
	N	N	$\frac{1}{8}$	$\times \frac{1}{3}$	=	$\frac{1}{24}$

The table shows all possibilities and the probabilities therefore total 1.0.

Probability of both vehicles being able to go 30 miles in any one day

= P (YY)

= $\frac{14}{24}$

Probability of at least one vehicle being able to go 30 miles in any one day

= P(YY) + P(YN) + P(NY)

= $\frac{14}{24}$ + $\frac{7}{24}$ + $\frac{2}{24}$ = $\frac{23}{24}$

Probability of only vehicle V being able to go 30 miles in any one day

= P(YN)

= $\frac{7}{24}$

Probability of exactly one vehicle being able to go 30 miles in any one day

= P(YN) + P(NY)

= $\frac{7}{24}$ + $\frac{2}{24}$ = $\frac{9}{24}$

36

The probability of at least one error is 100% minus the probability of no errors:

Probability = [1 - (0.85 x 0.80 x 0.70)] x 100% = 52.4%

Question

37 Using a table to record some of the possible results, where Y = Yes, N = No

Error made by worker			Probabilities		
1	*2*	*3*			
Y	N	N	0.15 x 0.80 x 0.70	=	0.084
N	Y	N	0.85 x 0.20 x 0.70	=	0.119
N	N	Y	0.85 x 0.80 x 0.30	=	0.204
Total probability					0.407
				=	40.7%

38 The probability of a toy being defective is 1 minus the probability of a toy not being defective. The probability of *not* being defective is 0.99 for each component, and therefore for all ten components is $(0.99)^{10}$.

Probability of a toy being defective = $1 - (0.99)^{10}$.

Distractor A gives the probability that all ten components are defective.

39 The probability of a product not being faulty is 0.8.

P(at least 3 not faulty) = P(3 not faulty + P(4 not faulty)

Therefore, we need to calculate first the probability of 3 products not being faulty.

Probability that one product will be faulty, and the other three not faulty

= 0.20 x 0.08 x 0.80 x 0.80
= 0.1024

Question

Number of combinations possible of one faulty and three not faulty

$$= {}_4C_3 \times \frac{4!}{1!\ 3!} = 4$$

Total probability of 3 products not being faulty = 4 x 0.1024 = 0.4096

P(at least 3 not faulty) = P(3 not faulty) + P(4 not faulty)
= 0.4096 + (0.8)^4
= 0.8192

40 P(at most one sale) = P(no sale or one sale)
= P(no sale) + P(one sale)

Calculate first the probability of making one sale:

The probability of making one sale out of five = $\frac{1}{3} \times (\frac{2}{3})^4$

The number of combinations possible of one sale and four 'no-sales'

$$= {}_5C_4 \times \frac{5!}{1!\ 4!} = 5$$

Total probability of making one sale = $5 \times \frac{1}{3} \times (\frac{2}{3})^4 = \frac{80}{243}$

P(at most one sale) = P(no sale) + P(one sale)

$$= (\frac{2}{3})^5 + \frac{80}{243}$$

$$= \frac{32}{243} + \frac{80}{243} = \frac{112}{243}$$

41 This is an example of the binomial distribution, because we have a number of identical trials, with a constant probability (0.6) of success (clearing 1.8m.)

n = 7
n = 3
p = 0.6

Probability = $\frac{7!}{(7-3)!\ 3!} \ 0.6^3 \ 0.4^4 = 0.194$

Question

42 Normal distribution tables are always set out in terms of standard deviations from the mean, so to get the answer, we must find how many standard deviations 26,000 words is above the mean of 20,000 words. 26,000 words is 6,000 words or one standard deviation above the mean. Tables (at the back of this book) give the proportion of values between the mean and one standard deviation above the mean as 0.3413. The proportion of values above the mean is 0.5, as the distribution is symmetrical. The proportion of values more than one standard deviation above the mean is therefore
0.5 - 0.3413 = 0.1587

43 From normal distribution tables, the required probability is 0.258 + 0.4641 = 0.7221.

44 £12,500 is £2,000 below the mean of £14,500 and 305/1,000 = 30.5% = 0.305 of the employees have salaries below £12,500. 0.5 - 0.305 = 0.195 of the employees have salaries between £12,500 and £14,500. We can look in normal distribution tables to find 0.195 in the body of the table, then see how many standard deviations away from the mean this corresponds to.

We find 0.195 at 0.51 standard deviations away from the mean, so £2,000 must be 0.51 standard deviations.

Standard deviation = $\dfrac{£2,000}{0.51}$ = £3,922

45 The normal distribution is a suitable approximation to use, because n is large and p is fairly close to 0.5.

Mean = np = 300 x 0.4 = 120

Standard deviation = $\sqrt{npq}$ = $\sqrt{300 \times 0.4 \times 0.6}$ = 8.485

125 is $\dfrac{125 - 120}{8.485}$ = 0.59 standard deviations above the mean.

From normal distribution tables (at the end of this book), the required probability is
0.5 - 0.2224 = 0.2776.

Question

46

Since n is large and p is near 0.5, the normal approximation to the binomial distribution is appropriate.

Mean = np = 150 x 0.45 = 67.5

Standard deviation = $\sqrt{npq}$ = $\sqrt{150 \times 0.45 \times 0.55}$ = $\sqrt{37.125}$ = 6.093

62 wins is $\frac{67.5 - 62}{6.093}$ = 0.90 standard deviations below the mean.

70 wins is $\frac{70 - 67.5}{6.093}$ = 0.41 standard deviations above the mean.

From normal distribution tables,
Area between the mean and 0.90 standard deviations away from the mean = 0.3159
Area between the mean and 0.41 standard deviations away from the mean = 0.1591
Required probability = 0.475

47

We get the numbers we need from Poisson distribution tables (at the end of this book), using the row for a mean of 2.2. P(3 or more calls) = 1 - P(0 or 1 or 2 calls) =
1 - (0.1108 + 0.2438 + 0.2681)
= 1 - 0.6227 = 0.3773

48

If the mean number of defects per km is 0.8, the mean number of defects per 3km is 0.8 x 3 = 2.4.

We can now look up the probability of 4 occurrences in Poisson tables, using the row for a mean of 2.4. The tables give a probability of 0.1254.

49

The Poisson distribution is a suitable approximation, because n is large and p is small. The mean is 500 x 0.0032 = 1.6. The required probability, from tables, is 0.323 + 0.2584 = 0.5814

50

We want an interval such that if we say the mean weight of all women falls within that interval, we have a 95% chance of being right.

Confidence interval = 53 kg ± 1.96 x $\frac{12 \text{ kg}}{\sqrt{50}}$ = 53 kg ± 3.33 kg

= 49.67 kg to 56.33 kg

Question

51

The 95% confidence interval is

$$\text{Sample mean} \pm 1.96 \times \frac{\sigma}{\sqrt{n}}$$

We require that $1.96 \times \frac{\sigma}{\sqrt{n}}$ be not more than 2g. We therefore have

$$1.96 \times \frac{15}{\sqrt{n}} = 2$$

$$\sqrt{n} = \frac{1.96 \times 15}{2} = 14.7$$

$$n = (14.7)^2 = 216.09,$$

which should be rounded up to 217 to ensure we get at least the required precision.

This sort of calculation saves us from doing unnecessary work by taking a larger sample than we need. Note that if we had wanted a narrower confidence interval, we would have needed a larger sample

52

The sample proportion is $36/80 = 0.45$. We want to give an interval such that if we say that the population proportion falls within it, we have a 99% chance of being right

$$\text{Confidence interval} = 0.45 \pm 2.58 \times \sqrt{\frac{0.45 \times 0.55}{80}} = 0.45 \pm 0.144$$

53

The decision to continue at point Q has an expected value of

$$(\pounds70m \times 0.6) - (\pounds30m \times 0.4) = \pounds30m$$

The decision to abandon has a certain profit outcome of £65m, which is therefore the expected value, as at point Q the decision to abandon should be taken.

54

The decision to continue at point R has an expected value of

$$(\pounds100m \times 0.2) - (\pounds5m \times 0.8) = \pounds16m$$

This exceeds the profit of £15m from abandonment, therefore £16m is the expected value.

55

The expected value of option Y
$$= (\text{EV at point Q} \times 0.7 + \text{EV at point R} \times 0.3)$$
$$= \pounds65m \times 0.7 + \pounds16m \times 0.3$$
$$= \pounds50.3m$$

Question

56 The expected value at Z = (£100m x 0.7) + (£60m x 0.1) + (£30m x 0.2)
= £82m
less the cost of marketing   £50m
expected value of marketing   £32m

This exceeds the EV from abandonment, so the expected value is £32m.

57 The expected value at W   = (0.5 x EV at X + 0.5 x EV at Y)
= 0.5 x £32m + 0.5 x £24m
= £28m
Less cost of further research   £5m
= expected value of the decision   ——
to carry out further research   £23m

7: MARKING SCHEDULE

Question	Correct answer	Marks for correct answer	Question	Correct answer	Marks for correct answer	Question	Correct answer	Marks for correct answer
1	A	1	17	B	1	33	A	1
2	C	1	18	C	1	34	D	1
3	A	1	19	B	1	35	C	1
4	C	1	20	C	1	36	D	2
5	D	1	21	C	1	37	B	1
6	C	1	22	D	2	38	C	1
7	C	1	23	D	1	39	A	2
8	B	1	24	C	1	40	B	1
9	B	1	25	A	1	41	C	1
10	C	1	26	C	1	42	A	1
11	B	1	27	A	1	43	D	2
12	A	1	28	A	1	44	A	1
13	C	1	29	C	1	45	D	1
14	D	1	30	C	1	46	B	1
15	B	1	31	B	1			
16	C	1	32	A	1			

YOUR MARKS

Total marks available   50   Your total mark

7: MARKING SCHEDULE

GUIDELINES - If your mark was:

0 - 14
You are obviously having problems with these topics. Go back to your study text and then try the questions again.

25 - 36
Good. You are still making some mistakes, but you can calculate most of the averages and measures of dispersion. Check whether any particular topics are causing you difficulty.

15 - 24
Still a number of weaknesses. Think carefully about the reasons for your errors and then try the questions again

37 - 50
Very good. You have a thorough understanding of the material in this chapter.

COMMENTS

Question

1

Arithmetic mean $= \dfrac{\Sigma x}{n} = \dfrac{8 + y - 15 - y + 22}{5} = \dfrac{15}{5} = 3$

2

Total sales in January to April	$= 4$ months x 44 units
	$= 176$ units
Total sales in January to June	$= (176 + 58 + 48)$ units
	$= 282$ units
Arithmetic mean	$= \dfrac{282}{6}$ units
	$= 47$ units

3

Arithmetic mean $= \dfrac{\Sigma x}{n} = \dfrac{q^2 + 4q + 42}{9} = 7$

Multiply by 9,

$$q^2 + 4q + 42 = 63$$
$$q^2 + 4q - 21 = 0$$
$$(q + 7)\ (q - 3) = 0$$
$$q = -7 \text{ or } 3$$

Since q is positive, the value of q is 3

4

The number of employees in department $3 = 100 - (54 + 22) = 24$. Let the arithmetic mean output per employee per month for department 3 be p. Since the arithmetic mean output per employee per month for all employees is 139 units:

Department 1		Department 2		Department 3		All departments
(130×54)	$+$	(22×160)	$+$	$(24 \times p)$	$=$	(100×139)
		$7{,}020 + 3{,}520 + 24p$			$=$	$13{,}900$
				$24p$	$=$	$3{,}360$
				p	$=$	140

The arithmetic mean output per employee per month for department 3 is 140 units.

Question

5

Since the arithmetic mean is equal to $\frac{\Sigma x}{n}$, the sum of the original fifteen numbers $= 20$

The sum of the original fifteen numbers $= 15 \times 20 = 300$

$$\frac{300 + N}{16} = 22$$

$$300 + N = 16 \times 22 = 352$$
$$N = 352 - 300$$
$$= 52$$

6

The company budgets to achieve the same total sales revenue from each product. We could select any sales revenue as the basis of our calculations - we have chosen a value of £240 per product. How many units of each product will earn £240 revenue?

Product	Units		Unit price		Sales revenue £
1	16	x	£15	=	240
2	15	x	£16	=	240
3	10	x	£24	=	240
	41				720

This gives us the required mix of the products, and the arithmetic mean selling price is equal to $\frac{£720}{41} = £17.56$.

7

To calculate the arithmetic mean of a grouped frequency distribution, we need to take the mid-point of each class interval:

Distance travelled per day

at least	less than	mid-point (x)	frequency (f)	fx
0	5	2.5	5	12.5
5	10	7.5	10	75.0
10	20	15.0	8	120.0
20	30	25.0	2	50.0
			$\Sigma f = 25$	$\Sigma fx = 257.5$

Arithmetic mean $= \frac{\Sigma fx}{\Sigma f} = \frac{257.5}{25} = 10.3$ miles

8

Time taken for the outward journey	$= \frac{15 \text{ kilometres}}{60 \text{ kph}}$	$= 0.25$ hour
Time taken for the inward journey	$= \frac{15 \text{ kilometres}}{20 \text{ kph}}$	$= 0.75$ hour
Time for total return journey of 30 km		$= 1.00$ hour

Mean speed over total return journey $= 30$km $\div$ 1 hour $= 30$ kilometres per hour

Question

9 We could use any journey distance between customers as the basis for our calculations. We will take 150 kilometres:

Time taken between customers 1 and 2 $= \dfrac{150}{30} = $ 5.0 hours

Time taken between customers 2 and 3 $= \dfrac{150}{60} = $ 2.5 hours

Time taken between customers 3 and 4 $= \dfrac{150}{50} = $ 3.0 hours

Total time taken for all three journeys (450 kilometres) $= $ 10.5 hours

Mean speed over all 3 journeys $= \dfrac{450}{10.5} = $ 42.9 kph

Any selected distance between customers will get the same answer.

10 The median is the middle number in a set of numbers once they have been ranked in order:

20, 20, 30, 40, 60, 70, 70, 70, 70

median = 60

11 Once more, the numbers must be ranked in order:

0, 0, 0, 3, 3, 5, 8, 9, 11, 11

median

The median occurs between the fifth and sixth items: $\dfrac{3 + 5}{2} = 4$

12 To find the median value, we need to calculate the cumulative frequency:

Number of jobs since leaving school	Frequency	Cumulative frequency
0	1	1
1	11	12
2	16	28 ← median
3	1	29
4	17	46
5	3	49
6	6	55

The median item is the $\dfrac{55 + 1}{2} = $ 28th item, which has a value of 2.

Question

13

The mode is the most frequently occurring number of jobs, which is 4.

14

The median is found by ranking the earnings in ascending or descending order:

	Earnings	Frequency	Cumulative frequency
	£		
Shelf filler	6,000	3	3
Checkout operator	7,000	4	7
Supervisor	10,000	2	9 ← median
Storekeeper	11,000	2	11
Administrator	12,000	3	14
Manager	15,000	1	15

The median item is the $\frac{15+1}{2}$ = 8th item, which has a value of £10,000.

15

The modal class, the class interval with the highest frequency, is $\geq 25 < 40$.

Using the formula:

$$\text{Mode} = L + \frac{(F_1 - F_0) \times c}{2F_1 - F_0 - F_2}$$

where
L = lower limit of modal class = 25
F_0 = frequency of the next class below the modal class = 6
F_1 = frequency of the modal class = 19
F_2 = frequency of the next class above the modal class = 12
c = width of the modal class = 15

Our estimate of the mode would be:

$$25 + \frac{(19 - 6) \times 15}{38 - 6 - 12}$$

$$= 25 + \frac{195}{20}$$

$$= 25 + 9.75 = £34.75$$

Question

16 The median is the $\frac{47+1}{2}$ = 24th invoice. This invoice is in the class interval $\geqslant 25 < 40$.

Using the formula:

$$\text{Median} = \text{value of lower limit of median class} + \left(\frac{R}{f} \times c\right)$$

where R = difference between 24th invoice and cumulative frequency up to the end of the preceding class = 24 - 6 = 18
       f = frequency of the median class = 19
      c = width of the median class = 15

$$\text{Median} = 25 + \left(\frac{(24\text{-}6)}{19} \times 15\right)$$
$$= 25 + 14.21 = \text{£}39.21$$

17 With 1,500 television sets in total, the median age will be the age of the 750th set in order. This can be found by drawing a line out from 750 until it meets the ogive, then drawing a line down from that point.

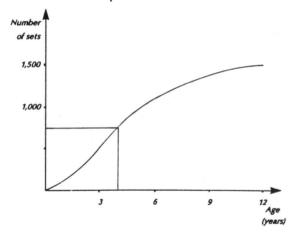

The median age is about 4 years.

Question

18

The approximate value of the mode may be found by drawing lines as shown below.

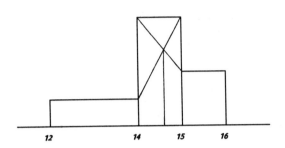

This is clearly to the right of the mid-point of the modal class, but not very near the upper limit of the class, so 14.625 is the correct answer.

19

The geometric mean price is equal to $\sqrt{£2.50 \times £3.60} = £3.00$

20

The geometric mean is equal to the fourth root of the product of the four numbers:

$$\sqrt[4]{8 \times 2p \times 1 \times p} = 10$$
$$8 \times 2p \times 1 \times p = 10^4$$
$$16p^2 = 10,000$$
$$p^2 = 625$$
$$p = 25$$

Question

21

In order to leave the geometric mean unaltered, N must be equal to the original mean = 10.

$$\sqrt{\text{Product of the original two numbers}} = 10$$

Product of the original two numbers $= 10^2 = 100$

$$\sqrt[3]{100 \times N} = 10$$

$100 \times N = 10^3 = 1,000$

$N = 10$

22

Value	Frequency	Cumulative frequency
1	1	1
2	1	2
3	3	5
6	6	11
7	8	19
10	9	28
11	8	36
15	5	41
20	3	44

Statement 1 is not correct. The lower quartile is the value of the 11th item, which is 6.

Statement 2 is not correct. The median is the arithmetic mean of the values of the 22nd and 23rd items, which is 10.

Statement 3 is correct. The upper quartile is the value of the 33rd item, which is 11.

23

Value of delivery (£) at least	less than	Frequency	Cumulative frequency
1	10	3	3
10	20	6	9
20	30	11	20
30	40	15	35
40	50	12	47
50	60	7	54
60	70	6	60

The lower quartile is the $\frac{1}{4} \times$ 60th = 15th item, which is in the class £20 to £30.

Continued...

Question

We use the formula:

$$\text{Quartile} = \text{value of lower limit of class} + \left(\frac{R}{f} \times c \right)$$

where R   is the quartile member minus the cumulative frequency up to the end of the preceding class = 15 - 9 = 6
       f   is the frequency of the quartile class = 11
       c   is the width of the quartile class = £10

$$\text{Lower quartile, } Q_1 = £20 + \left(\frac{15-9}{11} \times £10 \right)$$

$$= £20 + £5.45 = £25.45$$

24 The upper quartile is the $\frac{3}{4} \times$ 60th = 45th item. Using the cumulative frequencies in the last question, the 45th item is in the class interval £40 to £50.

Using the formula from the last question,   R   = 45 - 35 = 10
                                          f   = 12
                                          c   = 10

$$\text{Upper quartile, } Q_3 = £40 + \left(\frac{(45-35)}{12} \times £10 \right)$$

$$= £40 + £8.33 = £48, \text{ to the nearest } £$$

25 The quartile deviation is $\dfrac{Q_3 - Q_1}{2}$

where Q_3 = upper quartile   = £48.33
         Q_1 = lower quartile   = £25.45

$$\text{Quartile deviation} = \frac{£(48.33 - 25.45)}{2}$$

$$= £11, \text{ to the nearest } £$$

26 The quartile coefficient of dispersion $= \dfrac{Q_3 - Q_1}{Q_3 + Q_1}$

$$= \frac{£(48.33 - 25.45)}{£(48.33 + 25.45)}$$

$$= \frac{£22.88}{£73.78} = 0.31$$

This indicates that the distribution is moderately spread out (dispersed).

Question

27 To find the mean deviation, we first need to calculate the arithmetic mean (the first three columns of the following table):

Number of breakdowns x	Number of machines f	fx	$\|x - \bar{x}\|$	$f\|x - \bar{x}\|$
6	8	48	2.4	19.2
7	12	84	1.4	16.8
8	20	160	0.4	8.0
9	22	198	0.6	13.2
10	16	160	1.6	25.6
11	2	22	2.6	5.2
	$\Sigma f = 80$	$\Sigma fx = 672$		88.0

Arithmetic mean $= \bar{x} = \dfrac{\Sigma fx}{\Sigma f} = \dfrac{672}{80} = 8.4$ breakdowns.

The significance of the vertical bars in $\|x - \bar{x}\|$ is that negative signs are ignored.

Mean deviation $= \dfrac{\Sigma f\|x - \bar{x}\|}{n} = \dfrac{88}{80} = 1.1$ breakdowns

28 The coefficient of mean deviation is simply the mean deviation expressed as a proportion of the arithmetic mean:

$$\dfrac{\text{Mean deviation}}{\text{Arithmetic mean}} = \dfrac{1.1}{8.4} = 0.13$$

29

Mid-point of class (x)	Frequency (f)	fx	$\|x - \bar{x}\|$	$f\|x - \bar{x}\|$
50	10	500	162	1,620
150	11	1,650	62	682
250	17	4,250	38	646
350	12	4,200	138	1,656
	$\Sigma f = 50$	$\Sigma fx = 10,600$		4,604

$\bar{x} = \dfrac{\Sigma fx}{\Sigma f} = \dfrac{10,600}{50} = 212$

Mean deviation $= \dfrac{\Sigma f\|x - \bar{x}\|}{\Sigma f} = \dfrac{£4,604}{50} = £92.08$

Question

30

The arithmetic mean of the five numbers, $\bar{x}$, is equal to $\dfrac{4+6+8+12+15}{5} = \dfrac{45}{5} = 9$

We can now calculate the variance:

x	$x - \bar{x}$	$(x - \bar{x})^2$
4	-5	25
6	-3	9
8	-1	1
12	3	9
15	6	36
	$\Sigma f(x - \bar{x})^2 =$	80

Variance $= \dfrac{\Sigma (x-\bar{x})^2}{n} = \dfrac{80}{5} = 16$

31

The arithmetic mean of the seven ages, $\bar{x}$ is equal to $\dfrac{4+5+6+8+10+11+12}{7} = \dfrac{56}{7} = 8$

We can now calculate the standard deviation

x	$x - \bar{x}$	$(x - \bar{x})^2$
4	-4	16
5	-3	9
6	-2	4
8	0	0
10	2	4
11	3	9
12	4	16
	$\Sigma (x - \bar{x})^2 =$	58

Sample standard deviation $= s = \sqrt{\dfrac{(x - \bar{x})^2}{n}} = \sqrt{\dfrac{58}{7}} = \sqrt{8.286} = 2.88$

Since this is a small sample, Bessel's correction can make a significant difference, so it should be applied in finding σ.

Estimated population standard deviation $= \sigma = s\sqrt{\dfrac{n}{n-1}} = 2.88\sqrt{\dfrac{7}{6}} = 3.11$

32

Using Bessel's correction, the population standard deviation is equal to $\sqrt{\dfrac{n}{n-1}} \times$ the sample standard deviation. Therefore, the population variance (the square of the population standard deviation) is equal to $\dfrac{n}{n-1} \times$ the sample variance.

Question

33

Mid-point of invoice value (x)	Number of invoices (f)	fx
10	4	40
30	7	210
50	6	300
70	2	140
90	6	540
	$\Sigma f = 25$	$\Sigma fx = 1,230$

Arithmetic mean $= \dfrac{\Sigma fx}{\Sigma f} = \dfrac{1,230}{25} = £49.20$

34 We use the arithmetic mean, $\bar{x} = £49.20$ as calculated in the previous question.

Mid-point of invoice value (x)	Number of invoices (f)	$(x - \bar{x})$	$(x - \bar{x})^2$	$f(x - \bar{x})^2$
10	4	-39.20	1,536.64	6,146.56
30	7	-19.20	368.64	2,580.48
50	6	0.80	0.64	3.84
70	2	20.80	432.64	865.28
90	6	40.80	1,664.64	9,987.84
	$\Sigma f = 25$			$\Sigma f(x - \bar{x})^2 = 19,584.00$

Sample variance $= s^2 = \dfrac{f(x - \bar{x})^2}{n} = \dfrac{19,584}{25} = £783.36.$

Estimated population variance $= \sigma^2 = s^2 \times \dfrac{n}{n-1} = 783.36 \times \dfrac{25}{24} = £816.00$

35 The formula for the coefficient of variation is: $\dfrac{\text{Standard deviation}}{\text{Mean}}$

Distribution	Coefficient of variation
1	0.24
2	0.25
3	0.35 ←——— largest
4	0.21

36 If everybody's wage rises by 16%, the mean wage will also rise by 16%. In computing the standard deviation, we work out $(x - \bar{x})^2$ for each employee, add up the results, divide by n and then take the square root. If each employee's wage and the mean wage are all increased by 16%, each $(x - \bar{x})$ will rise by 16%. Because the squaring is followed by square rooting, the overall effect will be to increase the standard deviation by 16%.

Since both the standard deviation and the mean increase by 16%, the coefficient of variation, which is the one divided by the other, will be unchanged.

Question

37   We want the standard deviation of a total. We cannot add standard deviations, so 7.3 x 5 = 36.5 is wrong, but we can find the daily variance, add five days' variances to get the variance for the week, and take the square root to get to the standard deviation for the week.

The variance of the daily demand = (Standard deviation)^2
                                  = 7.3 x 7.3
                                  = 53.29
Variance for a 5 day week = 53.29 x 5
                          = 266.45
Standard deviation for a 5 day week = $\sqrt{266.45}$ = 16.3 units

38   The variance of X + Y + Z = $(0.4)^2 + (0.1)^2 + (0.7)^2$
                                  = 0.66
Standard deviation of
X + Y + Z = $\sqrt{0.66}$ = 0.8 kg

39

x	y	x^2	y^2	xy
4	12	16	144	48
3	15	9	225	45
1	10	1	100	10
3	14	9	196	42
11	51	35	665	145

$$r = \frac{n\Sigma xy - \Sigma x \Sigma y}{\sqrt{[n\Sigma x^2 - (\Sigma x)^2][n\Sigma y^2 - (\Sigma y)^2]}}$$

$$= \frac{4 \times 145 - 11 \times 55}{\sqrt{[4 \times 35 - 11^2][4 \times 665 - 51^2]}}$$

$$= \frac{-25}{\sqrt{1,121}} = -0.75$$

This indicates that as one variable rises, the other tends to fall (r being negative), and that the connection between the variables is fairly strong.

40   The coefficient of determination is the required figure. $r^2 = 0.72^2 = 0.52$. This shows that only just over half of the variation in one variable is explained by variation in the other.

Question

41

$$r = \frac{\text{Covariance of x and y}}{(\text{Standard deviation of x})(\text{Standard deviation of y})}$$

$$= \frac{-20}{\sqrt{12}\ \sqrt{42}} = \frac{-20}{22.45} = -0.89$$

42

Student	d	d²
P	4	16
Q	0	0
R	1	1
S	3	9
T	2	4
		30

$$r_s = 1 - \frac{6\Sigma d^2}{n(n^2-1)} = 1 - \frac{6 \times 30}{5(5^2-1)} = 1 - \frac{150}{120} = -0.25.$$

43

x	y	x²	xy
0	3	0	0
1	4	1	4
2	6	4	12
3	13	5	16

$$b = \frac{n\Sigma xy - \Sigma x\Sigma y}{n\Sigma x^2 - (\Sigma x)^2} = \frac{3 \times 16 - 3 \times 13}{3 \times 5 - 3^2} = \frac{9}{6} = 1.5$$

$$a = \bar{y} - b\bar{x} = \frac{13}{3} - 1.5 \times \frac{3}{3} = 2.83$$

The regression line is y = 2.83 + 1.5x.

If the values of x and y were plotted on a graph, they would tend to lie along this line.

44

Predicted value of y = -32 + (0.7 × 48.5) = 1.95

Question

45 We must first compute b, then find a.

$$b = \frac{n\Sigma xy - \Sigma x \Sigma y}{n\Sigma x^2 - (\Sigma x)^2}$$

$$= \frac{20 \times 6{,}580 - 210 \times 500}{20 \times 2{,}870 - 210^2} = \frac{26{,}600}{13{,}300} = 2$$

$$a = \bar{y} - b\bar{x} = \frac{500}{20} - 2 \times \frac{210}{20} = 25 - 21 = 4.$$

46 $r = \sqrt{0.73 \times 1.02}$

$r^2 = 0.73 \times 1.02 = 0.7446 \simeq 0.74.$

8: MARKING SCHEDULE

Question	Correct answer	Marks for correct answer	Question	Correct answer	Marks for correct answer	Question	Correct answer	Marks for correct answer
1	C	1	16	D	2	31	B	2
2	B	1	17	C	2	32	B	1
3	C	1	18	D	2	33	C	1
4	C	1	19	B	1	34	C	1
5	B	1	20	C	1	35	C	1
6	B	1	21	B	1	36	B	1
7	A	1	22	C	1	37	C	1
8	A	1	23	D	1	38	D	1
9	D	1	24	B	1	39	A	1
10	A	1	25	C	1	40	C	1
11	B	1	26	D	1	41	C	1
12	B	1	27	C	1	42	B	2
13	A	1	28	B	1	43	D	2
14	D	1	29	C	1			
15	B	1	30	C	1			

YOUR MARKS

Total marks available   49   Your total mark

GUIDELINES - If your mark was:

0 - 14 You are obviously having a great deal of difficulty with these topics. Go back to your study text and work through it again carefully.

29 - 40 Quite good. Although there are still some gaps in your knowledge you have a sound grasp of the basic principles.

15 - 28 Still quite a few weaknesses. You need to do a little better.

41 - 49 Very good. You have a clear understanding of the essential principles of these fundamental topics.

244

COMMENTS

Question

1

To find the percentage increase since year 9, we must take the increase as a percentage of the year 9 value. The increase in the index of 18 points between year 9 and year 14 is therefore a percentage increase of (18/180 x 100%) = 10%.

2

Let the average annual percentage price increase be 100x%. Over five years, the index has increased from 180 to 198:

$$180(1 + x)^5 = 198$$

$$(1 + x)^5 = \frac{198}{180}$$

$$= 1.1$$

$$1 + x = \sqrt[5]{1.1}$$

$$= 1.019$$

$$x = 0.019$$

Annual percentage price increase = 1.9% (to one decimal place)

3

The year 2 price index $= \frac{120}{80} \times 100 = 150$

Note that the base year value (80) goes below the line, and not the year 2 value (120).

4

The year 5 quantity index $= \frac{25,000}{20,000} \times 100 = 125$

5

The weighting of the index is to be based on the proportions of total weekly wages incurred in year 1:

	£ per hour	Average weekly labour hours	Total weekly wages (£)	%
Unskilled	2	180	360	9.0
Semi-skilled	3	140	420	10.5
Skilled	4	805	3,220	80.5
			4,000	100.0

Unskilled wages represent 9% of the total, therefore this is the weighting to be applied.

245

Question

6   The price relative is the price of semi-skilled labour in year 4 expressed as a percentage of the price in the base year, year 1:

Price relative of semi-skilled labour $= \dfrac{£3.60}{£3.00} \times 100 = 120$

7   To answer the question we need to know the price relatives for the other grades of labour:

Price relative of unskilled labour $= \dfrac{£2.32}{£2.00} \times 100 = 116$

Price relative of skilled labour $= \dfrac{£4.40}{£4.00} \times 100 = 110$

Using the percentage weightings calculated in question 5:

Grade of labour	Weighting (i)	Price relative (ii)	(i) x (ii)
Unskilled	9.0%	116	10.44
Semi-skilled	10.5%	120	12.60
Skilled	80.5%	110	88.55
			111.59

To the nearest whole number, the index number for year 4 is 112.

This indicates a 12% rise in overall labour costs.

8   The value of commodities consumed in the base year, year 1, will be used as the basis of weighting:

	Total expenditure £	%
L 4,000 x £2	8,000	10
M 8,000 x £5	40,000	50
N 4,000 x £8	32,000	40
	80,000	100

We are already given the price relative, which is the year 3 price as a percentage of the year 1 price for each commodity. The price relatives multiplied by the weights give the correct price index:

	Price relative	Weight	
L	102	10%	10.2
M	90	50%	45.0
N	98	40%	39.2
		Price index for year 3	94.4

This indicates that overall, prices have fallen.

Question

9

Description A corresponds to a Laspeyre volume index;
Description B corresponds to a Paasche volume index;
Description C corresponds to a Laspeyre price index;
Description D corresponds to a Paasche price index.

10

The formula for the Laspeyre price index is $\dfrac{\Sigma p_1 q_0}{\Sigma p_0 q_0} \times 100$

	p_1	q_0	p_0	$p_1 q_0$	$p_0 q_0$
X	30	50	10	1,500	500
Y	16	90	12	1,440	1,080
Z	12	110	14	1,320	1,540
				4,260	3,120

Laspeyre price index for year 6 $= \dfrac{4,260}{3,120} \times 100 = 136.5$

This indicates that overall, prices have risen by 36.5%.

11

The formula for the Paasche price index is $\dfrac{\Sigma p_1 q_1}{\Sigma p_0 q_1} \times 100$

	p_1	q_1	p_0	$p_1 q_1$	$p_0 q_1$
X	30	80	10	2,400	800
Y	16	110	12	1,760	1,320
Z	12	130	14	1,560	1,820
				5,720	3,940

Paasche price index for year 6 $= \dfrac{5,720}{3,940} \times 100 = 145.2$

This indicates that overall, prices have risen by 45.2%. Note that this differs from the conclusion reached using the Laspeyre index, even though the data were exactly the same. This illustrates how different weights (here, year 6 quantities as against year 1 quantities) can give different results. We can safely conclude that overall, prices have risen by approximately 40%.

12

The first thing to notice is that we are given the sales *values* for the products, therefore we need to divide by the volumes to derive the prices which we need for the relevant indices.

$$\text{Laspeyre price index} = \frac{\Sigma p_1 q_1}{\Sigma p_0 q_1} \times 100$$

Continued...

Question

	p_1	q_0	p_0	$p_1 q_0$	$p_0 q_0$
F	14	4.5	12	63.0	54.0
G	11	3.1	8	34.1	24.8
H	7	6.8	2	47.6	13.6
				144.7	92.4

Laspeyre price index for year 8 = $\dfrac{144.7}{92.4}$ x 100 = 156.6

13 As with question 12, it is necessary to convert the sales values to sales prices.

Paasche price index = $\dfrac{\Sigma p_1 q_1}{\Sigma p_0 q_1}$ x 100

	p_1	q_1	p_0	$p_1 q_1$	$p_0 q_1$
F	14	6.8	12	95.2	81.6
G	11	4.1	8	45.1	32.8
H	7	8.6	2	60.2	17.2
				200.5	131.6

Paasche price index for year 8 = $\dfrac{200.5}{131.6}$ x 100 = 152.4

14 Once again, convert the relevant sales value figures to sales prices before calculating the indices.

Laspeyre volume index = $\dfrac{\Sigma q_1 p_0}{\Sigma q_0 p_0}$ x 100

	q_1	p_0	q_0	$q_1 p_0$	$q_0 p_0$
F	6.8	12	4.5	81.6	54.0
G	4.1	8	3.1	32.8	24.8
H	8.6	2	6.8	17.2	13.6
				131.6	92.4

Laspeyre volume index for year 8 = $\dfrac{131.6}{92.4}$ x 100 = 142.4

This indicates that overall, sales volume has risen by 42.4%.

248

Question

15 Paasche volume index $= \dfrac{\Sigma q_1 p_1}{\Sigma q_0 p_1} \times 100$

	q_1	p_0	q_0	$q_1 p_1$	$q_0 p_1$
F	6.8	14	4.5	95.2	63.0
G	4.1	11	3.1	45.1	34.1
H	8.6	7	6.8	60.2	47.6
				200.5	144.7

Paasche volume index for year 8 $= \dfrac{200.5}{144.7} \times 100 = 138.6$

This indicates that overall, sales volume has risen by 38.6%. As with price indices, Laspeyre and Paasche quantity or volume indices can give different results from the same data, and we should perhaps restrict ourselves to saying that sales volume has risen by about 40%.

16 While the subject matter of these two questions is productivity, rather than prices or volumes, the computations are on the same lines as for volume indices. The productivity ratios take the place of quantities, and the output volumes take the place of prices. A Laspeyre index would use the base year output volumes as the basis for weighting the productivity ratios for each department.

Department	(a) Year 2 productivity ratio (%)	(b) Year 1 output	(c) Year 1 productivity ratio (%)	(a x b)	(c x b)
1	97	28	104	2,716	2,912
2	106	40	98	4,240	3,920
				6,956	6,832

Laspeyre productivity index for year 2 $= \dfrac{6,956}{6,832} \times 100 = 101.8$

This indicates that in year 2, the two departments combined were slightly more productive than in year 1. Department 1's fall in productivity was more than made up for by department 2's rise in productivity.

249

Question

17

A Paasche index would use the latest year output volumes as the basis for weighting the productivity ratios for each department.

Department	(a) Year 2 productivity ratio (%)	(b) Year 2 output	(c) Year 1 productivity ratio (%)	(a x b)	(c x b)
1	97	35	104	3,395	3,640
2	106	38	98	4,028	3,724
				7,423	7,364

Paasche productivity index for year 2 = $\frac{7,423}{7,364}$ x 100 = 100.8

Again, a slight rise in productivity is indicated.

18

Statement 1 is not necessarily correct. The index numbers indicate the price of each material relative to its price in year 1. If in year 1 material R cost £1 per unit and material S cost £10 per unit, in year 12 material R would cost £2.50 per unit and material S would cost £20 per unit.

Statement 2 is not correct but statement 3 is correct. The index for R has risen by 150 points, or 150%. The index for S has risen by 100 points, or 100%. Therefore the percentage change in price of material R was 50% greater than the percentage change in price of material S.

19

The index increased by (530.5 - 500.6) = 29.9 points between January and April year 10. This represents a percentage increase of

$\frac{29.9}{500.6}$ x 100% = 6.0%

20

The index increased by (524.5 - 435.0) = 89.5 points between February year 9 and February year 10. The annual rate of inflation is therefore

$\frac{89.5}{435.0}$ x 100% = 20.6%

Question

21 Let the average annual rate of inflation over the two years be 100x%. If an item whose price moved exactly in line with inflation cost £408 in January year 9, its price two years later would be £408(1 + x)(1 + x) = £408(1 + x)². Its price would (in accordance with the index figures given) have risen to £500.60. We can therefore work out the average annual rate of inflation as follows.

$$408.0(1 + x)^2 = 500.6$$

$$(1 + x)^2 = \frac{500.6}{408.0}$$

$$1 + x = \sqrt{\frac{500.6}{408.0}}$$

$$= 1.108$$

$$x = 0.108$$

The average annual rate of inflation is 10.8%.

22 We can use the index numbers for March year 10 and February year 9.

Price of the item in March year 10 = £5 x $\frac{527.4}{435.0}$ = £6.06

In reality, very few prices change exactly in line with the Retail Prices Index. Most prices rise either more quickly or more slowly than the Index.

23 Deflated expenditure = Actual expenditure x $\frac{\text{January 1988 RPI}}{\text{July 1989 RPI}}$

$$= £12,780 \times \frac{103.3}{115.5} = £11,430$$

24 To get the increase in real terms, we must deflate the 19X6 expenditure to remove the effects of inflation. The 19X6 expenditure deflated to 19X3 salary levels is

$$£298,150 \times \frac{129.3}{152.7} = £252,461$$

The percentage increase in real terms is

$$\frac{252,461 - 227,900}{227,900} \times 100\% = 10.8\%$$

We could go on to enquire whether the employees have become better paid in real terms, or whether the company has increased its workforce and increased its expenditure on salaries for that reason.

Question

25 The four components of a time series are the trend, cyclical variations, seasonal variations and random variations. Totals must be divided by the appropriate figure to obtain the trend. The totals themselves are not a component of the time series.

26 Cyclical variations occur over a cycle longer than seasonal variations.

27 Seasonal variations occur over a cycle shorter than that of any cyclical variations. For example, seasonal variations may occur over a year, and cyclical variations over five years. However, seasonal variations could occur over (for example) a week or a month, rather than a year. They need not repeat exactly, but could vary in size from one year, month etc to the next. The data may be a combination not only of trend and seasonal variations, but also of residuals.

28 The seven-day total for a day will be made up of the data for the three days before that day, that day itself and the three days after that day.

Week	Day	Data	Seven-day total
1	Tuesday	44	
	Wednesday	57	
	Thursday	49	
	Friday	51	331
	Saturday	38	
	Sunday	42	
2	Monday	50	

The required total is 331. As this total includes one figure from each day of the week, it should not reflect the seasonal variations which affect individual days' figures.

29

Week	Day	Data	Five-day total	Five-day average
1	Tuesday	29		
	Wednesday	31		
	Thursday	28	144	28.8
	Friday	26		
2	Monday	30		

The required average is 144/5 = 28.8. This figure does not reflect seasonal variations, since it is based on one data item from each of the five days of the week. Dividing the total by five brings us back to a figure of the right size (since the total covered five days). The figure of 28.8 is a trend figure for Thursday of week 1.

252

Question

30 Sales vary according to the day of the week. For example, Tuesday is a day of very low sales and Wednesday is a day of very high sales. Therefore the most suitable moving average is one which covers one full weekly cycle, ie a five day moving average. A five day moving total centred on Thursday of week 2 must be calculated:

		Sales units	
Week 2	Tuesday	79	
	Wednesday	129	
	Thursday	95	← centre point.
	Friday	100	
Week 3	Monday	<u>107</u>	
Five day moving total		<u>510</u>	

Moving average = 510 ÷ 5 = 102 units.

This moving average of 102 units constitutes a trend figure. The fact that is is higher than the actual figure for Thursday of week 2 (95 units) reflects the fact that Thursday is a day of low sales.

31 We need to calculate as many trend figures as possible, then compare these with the actual results for each day. The differences are the seasonal variations.

		Moving total of 5 days' sales (units)	Moving average of 5 days' sales (units)	Actual sales (units)	Seasonal variation (units)
Week 1	Wednesday	490	98.0	119	+21.0
	Thursday	491	98.2	92	-6.2
	Friday	492	98.4	99	+0.6
Week 2	Monday	502	100.4	103	+2.6
	Tuesday	505	101.0	79	-22.0
	Wednesday	506	101.2	129	+27.8
	Thursday	510	102.0	95	-7.0
	Friday	511	102.2	100	-2.2
Week 3	Monday	512	102.4	107	+4.6
	Tuesday	512	102.4	80	-22.4
	Wednesday	519	103.8	130	+26.2

Next calculate the average seasonal variation for each day in the weekly cycle, using the individual seasonal variations calculated above.

	Monday	Tuesday	Wednesday	Thursday	Friday	Total
Week 1			+21.0	-6.2	+0.6	
Week 2	+2.6	-22.0	+27.8	-7.0	-2.2	
Week 3	<u>+4.6</u>	<u>-22.4</u>	<u>+26.2</u>	<u></u>	<u></u>	
	<u>+3.6</u>	<u>-22.2</u>	<u>+25.0</u>	<u>-6.6</u>	<u>-0.8</u>	-1.0

Continued...

Question

We make an adjustment of + 1.0 to reduce the total variation to zero. This is so that the seasonal variations between them balance out, and do not affect the total for a whole week. The adjustment is apportioned + 0.20 to each day, making an average variation of + 25.2 units for Wednesday, or + 25 to the nearest whole number.

32
-
33

Because we have an even number of seasons (four quarters) in each cycle we must get to our trend figure in stages. The total for any four quarters will be centred *between* the quarters and will not relate to a particular quarter. To overcome this difficulty, we take totals of pairs of four-quarter totals.

Quarter	Sales units	Total of four quarter's sales (units)	Total of eight quarter's sales (units)	Eight quarter averages = (units)
1	76			
2	90			
		322		
3	92		648	81.0
		326		
4	64			
1	80			

34

The average seasonal variation is calculated by taking the average for each season, and then adjusting each of them up or down to bring the total variation to nil. This adjustment ensures that the seasonal variations balance each other out.

	Spring	Summer	Autumn	Winter	Total
Year 1			+ 11.2	+ 23.5	
Year 2	-9.8	-28.1	+ 12.5	+ 23.7	
Year 3	-7.4	-26.3	+ 11.7		
Average variation	-8.6	-27.2	+ 11.8	+ 23.6	-0.4
Adjust total variation to nil	+ 0.1	+ 0.1	+ 0.1	+ 0.1	+ 0.4
					0.0
Estimated seasonal variation	-8.5	-27.1	+ 11.9	+ 23.7	

Question

35 We first compute a forecast trend figure for the third quarter of year 9, and then add the seasonal variation to get the forecast sales for that quarter.

	£'000
Forecast trend for the third quarter of year 9	
= 1,632 + (3 x 25)	1,707
Adjust for average seasonal variation	+ 29
Forecast sales for third quarter of year 9	1,736

36 This question is like the last one, but with a negative seasonal variation. The effect is to give a forecast sales figure which is less than the forecast trend figure.

	£'000
Forecast trend for the first quarter of year 10	
= 1,632 + (5 x 25)	1,757
Adjust for average seasonal variation	-18
Forecast sales for first quarter of year 10	1,739

37 The residual is the difference between:

		£'000
(i)	the sales result which would have been predicted by the trend line adjusted for the seasonal variation:	
	(1,632 + 25) - 18 = 1,657 - 18	1,639
and		
(ii)	the actual sales	1,634
	Residual	-5

38 All activities ending at a node must be completed before any activities starting at that node can begin.

39 The critical paths through networks are those with the greatest durations. Every network has at least one critical path. A network may have several such paths. A critical path need not contain more activities than non-critical paths. A critical path may contain a few long activities, while a non-critical path through the same network might contain many short activities.

Question

40

Because work J starts a day after worker H, he has 8 - 1 = 7 days in which do 3 + 2 = 5 days' work. He may therefore take 7 - 5 = 2 days off between activities F and G. The network is as follows:

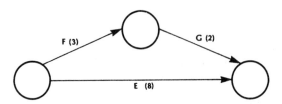

41

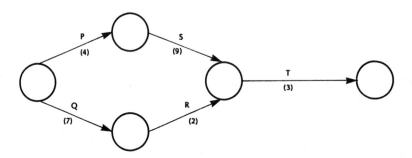

The paths are PST (4 + 9 + 3 = 16 days) and QRT (7 + 2 + 3 = 12 days). The minimum overall duration is 16 days.

Question

42

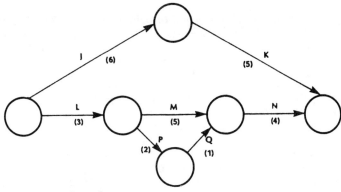

Path	Duration (days)
JK	11
LMN	12
LPQN	10

As LMN is the longest path, any delay on it would extend the duration of the whole project, so it is the critical path.

Note that LMPN is not a path through the network.

43

Activity	Mean duration	Standard deviation of duration	Variance of duration
X	3	0.33	0.11
Y	4.83	0.50	0.25
Z	9.83	0.83	0.69
	17.66		1.05

Mean durations are computed as $(o + 4m + p)/6$, and standard deviations as $(p-o)/6$. The standard deviation of the duration of the whole path is $\sqrt{1.05} = 1.025$. 19 days is $(19 - 17.66)/1.025 = 1.31$ standard deviations above the mean. The required probability is therefore (from normal distribution tables) $0.5 + 0.4049 = 0.9049 \simeq 0.9$.

PRESENT VALUE OF £1

The table shows the value of £1 to be received or paid after a given number of years.

Years	1%	2%	3%	4%	5%	6%	7%	8%	9%	10%	11%	12%
1	0.99	0.98	0.97	0.96	0.95	0.94	0.93	0.93	0.92	0.91	0.90	0.89
2	0.98	0.96	0.94	0.92	0.91	0.89	0.87	0.86	0.84	0.83	0.81	0.80
3	0.97	0.94	0.92	0.89	0.86	0.84	0.82	0.79	0.77	0.75	0.73	0.71
4	0.96	0.92	0.89	0.85	0.82	0.79	0.76	0.74	0.71	0.68	0.66	0.64
5	0.95	0.91	0.86	0.82	0.78	0.75	0.71	0.68	0.65	0.62	0.59	0.57
6	0.94	0.89	0.84	0.79	0.75	0.70	0.67	0.63	0.60	0.56	0.53	0.51
7	0.93	0.87	0.81	0.76	0.71	0.67	0.62	0.58	0.55	0.51	0.48	0.45
8	0.92	0.85	0.79	0.73	0.68	0.63	0.58	0.54	0.50	0.47	0.43	0.40
9	0.91	0.84	0.77	0.70	0.64	0.59	0.54	0.50	0.46	0.42	0.39	0.36
10	0.91	0.82	0.74	0.68	0.61	0.56	0.51	0.46	0.42	0.39	0.35	0.32
11	0.90	0.80	0.72	0.65	0.58	0.53	0.48	0.43	0.39	0.35	0.32	0.29
12	0.89	0.79	0.70	0.62	0.56	0.50	0.44	0.40	0.36	0.32	0.29	0.26
13	0.88	0.77	0.68	0.60	0.53	0.47	0.41	0.37	0.33	0.29	0.26	0.23
14	0.87	0.76	0.66	0.58	0.51	0.44	0.39	0.34	0.30	0.26	0.23	0.20
15	0.86	0.74	0.64	0.56	0.48	0.42	0.36	0.32	0.27	0.24	0.21	0.18

Years	13%	14%	15%	16%	17%	18%	19%	20%	30%	40%	50%
1	0.88	0.88	0.87	0.86	0.85	0.85	0.84	0.83	0.77	0.71	0.67
2	0.78	0.77	0.76	0.74	0.73	0.72	0.71	0.69	0.59	0.51	0.44
3	0.69	0.67	0.66	0.64	0.62	0.61	0.59	0.58	0.46	0.36	0.30
4	0.61	0.59	0.57	0.55	0.53	0.52	0.50	0.48	0.35	0.26	0.20
5	0.54	0.52	0.50	0.48	0.46	0.44	0.42	0.40	0.27	0.19	0.13
6	0.48	0.46	0.43	0.41	0.39	0.37	0.35	0.33	0.21	0.13	0.09
7	0.43	0.40	0.38	0.35	0.33	0.31	0.30	0.28	0.16	0.09	0.06
8	0.38	0.35	0.33	0.31	0.28	0.27	0.25	0.23	0.12	0.07	0.04
9	0.33	0.31	0.28	0.26	0.24	0.23	0.21	0.19	0.09	0.05	0.03
10	0.29	0.27	0.25	0.23	0.21	0.19	0.18	0.16	0.07	0.03	0.02
11	0.26	0.24	0.21	0.20	0.18	0.16	0.15	0.13	0.06	0.02	0.01
12	0.23	0.21	0.19	0.17	0.15	0.14	0.12	0.11	0.04	0.02	0.008
13	0.20	0.18	0.16	0.15	0.13	0.12	0.10	0.09	0.03	0.013	0.005
14	0.18	0.16	0.14	0.13	0.11	0.10	0.09	0.08	0.03	0.009	0.003
15	0.16	0.14	0.12	0.11	0.09	0.08	0.07	0.06	0.02	0.006	0.002

CUMULATIVE PV OF £1 (ANNUITY TABLES)

The table shows the present value of £1 per annum, receivable or payable at the end of each year for N years.

Years	1%	2%	3%	4%	5%	6%	7%	8%	9%	10%	11%	12%
1	0.99	0.98	0.97	0.96	0.95	0.94	0.94	0.93	0.92	0.91	0.90	0.89
2	1.97	1.94	1.91	1.89	1.86	1.83	1.81	1.78	1.76	1.74	1.71	1.69
3	2.94	2.88	2.83	2.78	2.72	2.67	2.62	2.58	2.53	2.49	2.44	2.40
4	3.90	3.81	3.72	3.63	3.55	3.47	3.39	3.31	3.24	3.17	3.10	3.04
5	4.85	4.71	4.58	4.45	4.33	4.21	4.10	3.99	3.89	3.79	3.70	3.61
6	5.80	5.60	5.42	5.24	5.08	4.92	4.77	4.62	4.49	4.36	4.23	4.11
7	6.73	6.47	6.23	6.00	5.79	5.58	5.39	5.21	5.03	4.87	4.71	4.56
8	7.65	7.33	7.02	6.73	6.46	6.21	5.97	5.75	5.54	5.34	5.15	4.97
9	8.57	8.16	7.79	7.44	7.11	6.80	6.52	6.25	6.00	5.76	5.54	5.33
10	9.47	8.98	8.53	8.11	7.72	7.36	7.02	6.71	6.42	6.15	5.89	5.65
11	10.37	9.79	9.25	8.76	8.31	7.89	7.50	7.14	6.81	6.50	6.21	5.94
12	11.26	10.58	9.95	9.39	8.86	8.38	7.94	7.54	7.16	6.81	6.49	6.19
13	12.13	11.35	10.64	9.99	9.39	8.85	8.36	7.90	7.49	7.10	6.80	6.42
14	13.00	12.11	11.30	10.56	9.90	9.30	8.75	8.24	7.79	7.37	6.98	6.63
15	13.87	12.85	11.94	11.12	10.38	9.71	9.11	8.56	8.06	7.61	7.19	6.81

Years	13%	14%	15%	16%	17%	18%	19%	20%	30%	40%	50%
1	0.89	0.88	0.87	0.86	0.85	0.85	0.84	0.83	0.77	0.71	0.67
2	1.67	1.65	1.63	1.61	1.59	1.57	1.55	1.53	1.36	1.22	1.11
3	2.36	2.32	2.28	2.25	2.21	2.17	2.14	2.11	1.81	1.59	1.41
4	2.97	2.91	2.86	2.80	2.74	2.69	2.64	2.59	2.17	1.85	1.61
5	3.52	3.43	3.35	3.27	3.20	3.13	3.06	2.99	2.44	2.04	1.74
6	4.00	3.89	3.78	3.69	3.59	3.50	3.41	3.33	2.64	2.17	1.82
7	4.42	4.29	4.16	4.04	3.92	3.81	3.71	3.61	2.80	2.26	1.88
8	4.80	4.64	4.49	4.34	4.21	4.08	3.95	3.84	2.93	2.33	1.92
9	5.13	4.95	4.77	4.61	4.45	4.30	4.16	4.03	3.02	2.38	1.95
10	5.43	5.22	5.02	4.83	4.66	4.49	4.34	4.19	3.09	2.41	1.97
11	5.69	5.45	5.23	5.03	4.83	4.66	4.49	4.33	3.15	2.44	1.98
12	5.92	5.66	5.42	5.20	4.99	4.79	4.61	4.44	3.19	2.46	1.99
13	6.12	5.84	5.58	5.34	5.12	4.91	4.71	4.53	3.22	2.47	1.99
14	6.30	6.00	5.72	5.47	5.23	5.01	4.80	4.61	3.25	2.48	1.99
15	6.46	6.14	5.85	5.58	5.32	5.09	4.88	4.68	3.27	2.48	2.00

POISSON DISTRIBUTION

Mean m	0	1	2	3	x 4	5	6	7	8
0.1	0.9048	0.0905	0.0045	0.0002	0.0000	0.0000	0.0000	0.0000	0.0000
0.2	0.8187	0.1637	0.0164	0.0011	0.0001	0.0000	0.0000	0.0000	0.0000
0.3	0.7408	0.2222	0.0333	0.0033	0.0003	0.0000	0.0000	0.0000	0.0000
0.4	0.6703	0.2681	0.0536	0.0072	0.0007	0.0001	0.0000	0.0000	0.0000
0.5	0.6065	0.3033	0.0758	0.0126	0.0016	0.0002	0.0000	0.0000	0.0000
0.6	0.5488	0.3293	0.0988	0.0198	0.0030	0.0004	0.0000	0.0000	0.0000
0.7	0.4966	0.3476	0.1217	0.0284	0.0050	0.0007	0.0001	0.0000	0.0000
0.8	0.4493	0.3595	0.1438	0.0383	0.0077	0.0012	0.0002	0.0000	0.0000
0.9	0.4066	0.3659	0.1647	0.0494	0.0111	0.0020	0.0003	0.0000	0.0000
1.0	0.3679	0.3679	0.1839	0.0613	0.0153	0.0031	0.0005	0.0001	0.0000
1.1	0.3329	0.3662	0.2014	0.0738	0.0203	0.0045	0.0008	0.0001	0.0000
1.2	0.3012	0.3614	0.2169	0.0867	0.0260	0.0062	0.0012	0.0002	0.0000
1.3	0.2725	0.3543	0.2303	0.0998	0.0324	0.0084	0.0018	0.0003	0.0001
1.4	0.2466	0.3452	0.2471	0.1128	0.0395	0.0111	0.0026	0.0005	0.0001
1.5	0.2231	0.3347	0.2510	0.1255	0.0471	0.0141	0.0035	0.0008	0.0001
1.6	0.2019	0.3230	0.2584	0.1378	0.0551	0.0176	0.0047	0.0011	0.0002
1.7	0.1827	0.3106	0.2640	0.1496	0.0636	0.0216	0.0061	0.0015	0.0003
1.8	0.1653	0.2975	0.2678	0.1607	0.0723	0.0260	0.0078	0.0020	0.0005
1.9	0.1496	0.2842	0.2700	0.1710	0.0812	0.0309	0.0098	0.0027	0.0006
2.0	0.1353	0.2707	0.2707	0.1804	0.0902	0.0361	0.0120	0.0034	0.0009
2.1	0.1225	0.2572	0.2700	0.1890	0.0992	0.0417	0.0146	0.0044	0.0011
2.2	0.1108	0.2438	0.2681	0.1966	0.1082	0.0476	0.0174	0.0055	0.0015
2.3	0.1003	0.2306	0.2652	0.2033	0.1169	0.0538	0.0206	0.0068	0.0019
2.4	0.0907	0.2177	0.2613	0.2090	0.1254	0.0602	0.0241	0.0083	0.0025
2.5	0.0821	0.2052	0.2565	0.2138	0.1336	0.0668	0.0278	0.0099	0.0031
2.6	0.0743	0.1931	0.2510	0.2176	0.1414	0.0735	0.0319	0.0118	0.0038
2.7	0.0672	0.1815	0.2450	0.2205	0.1488	0.0804	0.0362	0.0139	0.0047
2.8	0.0608	0.1703	0.2384	0.2225	0.1557	0.0872	0.0407	0.0163	0.0057
2.9	0.0550	0.1596	0.2314	0.2237	0.1622	0.0940	0.0455	0.0188	0.0068
3.0	0.0498	0.1494	0.2240	0.2240	0.1680	0.1008	0.0504	0.0216	0.0081
3.1	0.0450	0.1397	0.2165	0.2237	0.1733	0.1075	0.0555	0.0246	0.0095
3.2	0.0408	0.1304	0.2087	0.2226	0.1781	0.1140	0.0608	0.0278	0.0111
3.3	0.0369	0.1217	0.2008	0.2209	0.1823	0.1203	0.0662	0.0312	0.0129
3.4	0.0334	0.1135	0.1929	0.2186	0.1858	0.1264	0.0716	0.0348	0.0148
3.5	0.0302	0.1057	0.1850	0.2158	0.1888	0.1322	0.0771	0.0385	0.0169
3.6	0.0273	0.0984	0.1771	0.2125	0.1912	0.1377	0.0826	0.0425	0.0191
3.7	0.0247	0.0915	0.1692	0.2087	0.1931	0.1429	0.0881	0.0466	0.0215
3.8	0.0224	0.0850	0.1615	0.2046	0.1944	0.1477	0.0936	0.0508	0.0241
3.9	0.0202	0.0789	0.1539	0.2001	0.1951	0.1522	0.0989	0.0551	0.0269
4.0	0.0183	0.0733	0.1465	0.1954	0.1954	0.1563	0.1042	0.0595	0.0298
4.1	0.0166	0.0679	0.1393	0.1904	0.1951	0.1600	0.1093	0.0640	0.0328

NORMAL DISTRIBUTION

	0·00	0·01	0·02	0·03	0·04	0·05	0·06	0·07	0·08	0·09
0·0	·0000	·0040	·0080	·0120	·0159	·0199	·0239	·0279	·0319	·0359
0·1	·0398	·0438	·0478	·0517	·0557	·0596	·0636	·0675	·0714	·0753
0·2	·0793	·0832	·0871	·0910	·0948	·0987	·1026	·1064	·1103	·1141
0·3	·1179	·1217	·1255	·1293	·1331	·1368	·1406	·1443	·1480	·1517
0·4	·1554	·1591	·1628	·1664	·1700	·1736	·1772	·1808	·1844	·1879
0·5	·1915	·1950	·1985	·2019	·2054	·2088	·2123	·2157	·2190	·2224
0·6	·2257	·2291	·2324	·2357	·2389	·2422	·2454	·2486	·2518	·2549
0·7	·2580	·2611	·2642	·2673	·2704	·2734	·2764	·2794	·2823	·2852
0·8	·2881	·2910	·2939	·2967	·2995	·3023	·3051	·3078	·3106	·3133
0·9	·3159	·3186	·3212	·3238	·3264	·3289	·3315	·3340	·3365	·3389
1·0	·3413	·3438	·3461	·3485	·3508	·3531	·3554	·3577	·3599	·3621
1·1	·3643	·3665	·3686	·3708	·3729	·3749	·3770	·3790	·3810	·3830
1·2	·3849	·3869	·3888	·3907	·3925	·3944	·3962	·3980	·3997	·4015
1·3	·4032	·4049	·4066	·4082	·4099	·4115	·4131	·4147	·4162	·4177
1·4	·4192	·4207	·4222	·4236	·4251	·4265	·4279	·4292	·4306	·4319
1·5	·4332	·4345	·4357	·4370	·4382	·4394	·4406	·4418	·4430	·4441
1·6	·4452	·4463	·4474	·4485	·4495	·4505	·4515	·4525	·4535	·4545
1·7	·4554	·4564	·4573	·4582	·4591	·4599	·4608	·4616	·4625	·4633
1·8	·4641	·4649	·4656	·4664	·4671	·4678	·4686	·4693	·4699	·4706
1·9	·4713	·4719	·4726	·4732	·4738	·4744	·4750	·4756	·4762	·4767
2·0	·4772	·4778	·4783	·4788	·4793	·4798	·4803	·4808	·4812	·4817
2·1	·4821	·4826	·4830	·4834	·4838	·4842	·4846	·4850	·4854	·4857
2·2	·4861	·4865	·4868	·4871	·4875	·4878	·4881	·4884	·4887	·4890
2·3	·4893	·4896	·4898	·4901	·4904	·4906	·4909	·4911	·4913	·4916
2·4	·4918	·4920	·4922	·4925	·4927	·4929	·4931	·4932	·4934	·4936
2·5	·4938	·4940	·4941	·4943	·4945	·4946	·4948	·4949	·4951	·4952
2·6	·4953	·4955	·4956	·4957	·4959	·4960	·4961	·4962	·4963	·4964
2·7	·4965	·4966	·4967	·4968	·4969	·4970	·4971	·4972	·4973	·4974
2·8	·4974	·4975	·4976	·4977	·4977	·4978	·4979	·4980	·4980	·4981
2·9	·4981	·4982	·4983	·4983	·4984	·4984	·4985	·4985	·4986	·4986
3·0	·49865	·4987	·4987	·4988	·4988	·4989	·4989	·4989	·4990	·4990
3·1	·49903	·4991	·4991	·4991	·4992	·4992	·4992	·4992	·4993	·4993
3·2	·49931	·4993	·4994	·4994	·4994	·4994	·4994	·4995	·4995	·4995
3·3	·49952	·4995	·4995	·4996	·4996	·4996	·4996	·4996	·4996	·4997
3·4	·49966	·4997	·4997	·4997	·4997	·4997	·4997	·4997	·4997	·4998
3·5	·49977									

Further information

The Password series includes the following titles:

	Order code	
Economics	P01X	EC
Basic accounting	P028	BA
Financial accounting	P036	FA
Costing	P044	CO
Foundation business mathematics	P052	FB
Business law	P060	BL
Auditing	P079	AU
Organisation and management	P087	OM
Advanced business mathematics	P095	AB
Taxation	P109	TX
Management accounting	P117	MA
Interpretation of accounts	P125	IA
Financial management	P133	FM
Company law	P141	CL
Information technology	P15X	IT

Password is available from most major bookshops. If you have any difficulty obtaining them, please contact BPP directly, quoting the above order codes.

BPP Publishing Limited
Aldine Place
142/144 Uxbridge Road
London W12 8AA

Tel: 01-740 1111
Fax: 01-740 1184
Telex: 265871 (MONREF G) - quoting '76:SJJ098'